Marjorie McCann Collier

Siamese Cats

Everything about Acquisition, Care,
Nutrition, Behavior, Health Care, and Breeding

With 27 Photographs

Illustrations by Michele Earle-Bridges

BARRON'S

Credits/Contents

Photo Credits: Ju Binville: page 28 (bottom left); Chanan: inside front cover, pages 9 (bottom), 10 (top), 27 (top), 28 (top, bottom right), 45, 46 (top right, bottom), back cover (bottom right); Marjorie Collier: back cover (top-right—lilac-point female, Ch. Tanuk Sweet Mystery with four-week-old kittens, breeder/owner Marjorie Collier); Gary W. Ellis: front cover, pages 63 (top right, bottom), 64, inside back cover; Susan Green: back cover (bottom left); Rob Lauwers: pages 10 (bottom), 63 (top left), back cover (top left); B. Everett Webb (Natures Moments): pages 9 (top), 27 (bottom), 46 (top left).

About the Author: Marjorie McCann Collier and her husband share their Brooklyn, New York home with several Siamese. Dr. Collier, a professor of biology at Saint Peter's College in New Jersey, has lived with Siamese for nearly forty years and has bred and shown them for more than twenty. She is an all-breed judge for the Cat Fanciers' Federation, Inc. in the United States and has served as guest judge in Canada and Europe. The Colliers also rescue, rehabilitate, and find homes for stray cats and dogs, with the help of their veterinarian, friends, and humane societies.

All inquiries should be addressed to:
Barron's Educational Series, Inc.
250 Wireless Boulevard
Hauppauge, NY 11788

International Standard Book No. 0-8120-4764-8

Library of Congress Catalog Card No. 91-34768

Library of Congress Cataloging-in-Publication Data

Collier, Marjorie McCann.
    Siamese cats : everything about acquisition, care, nutrition, behavior, health care, and breeding / Marjorie McCann Collier ; illustrations by Michele Earle-Bridges.
        p.   cm.
    Includes bibliographical references and index.
    ISBN 0-8120-4764-8
    1. Siamese cat. I. Earle-Bridges, Michele. II. Title.
SF449.S5C65   1991
636.8'25—dc20   91-34768
                                                          CIP

PRINTED IN HONG KONG
2345   4900   098765432

Contents/Foreword

My first impression of a Siamese was from a book on breeds of cats (title long forgotten); I turned the page and there was this triangular face with dark mask, too-tall ears, and slanty blue eyes. My instantaneous reaction was, "This is the ugliest cat I've ever seen, and I have to have one!" Fortunately, my mother, for I was in my midteens then, agreed, and not long after, I got my first of many Siamese. Needless to say, my opinion about their ugliness was soon changed. They have also taught me reams about cats in general and their breed in particular, while giving me unlimited entertainment, companionship, and love.

In this book I want to share my most important lessons from the Siamese with those who have recently acquired a Siamese or are thinking of getting one.

Acknowledgments: The author thanks her family (human and feline) and the Brooklyn Cat Fanciers for their encouragement and support. Thanks are also due Helgard Niewisch DVM for her careful reading of the manuscript.

Important Note: When you handle cats you may sometimes get scratched or bitten. If this happens, have a doctor treat the injuries immediately.

Make sure your cat receives all the necessary shots and wormings, otherwise serious danger to the animal and to human health may arise. A few diseases and parasites can be communicated to humans. If your cat shows any signs of illness, you should definitely consult a veterinarian. If you are worried about your own health, see your doctor and tell him or her that you have cats.

Some people have allergic reactions to cat hair. If you think you might be allergic, ask your doctor before you get a cat.

It is possible for a cat to cause damage to someone else's property and even to cause accidents. For your own protection you should make sure your insurance covers such eventualities, and you should definitely have liability insurance.

What Is a Siamese?

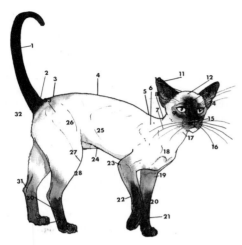

The external anatomy of the Siamese cat.

1. tail	13. forehead	23. elbow
2. base of tail	14. eyes	24. belly
3. rump	15. nose	25. rib cage
4. back	16. whiskers	26. upper thigh
5. withers	17. throat	27. knee joint
6. shoulder	18. chest	28. lower thigh
7. neck	19. upper arm	29. pads
8. nape of neck	20. lower arm	30. metatarsus
9. cheeks	21. metacarpus	31. hock
10. occiput	22. middle	32. anal region
11. ears	portion,	33. hip
12. crown	front foot	

Superficial musculature. The many ways in which the muscles cross the joints allow fine and complex movements.

The skull. The large size of the eye sockets and jaws are characteristics of night hunters. The molars, which are called carnassials, work like scissors in cutting off pieces of food, instead of grinders as in humans.

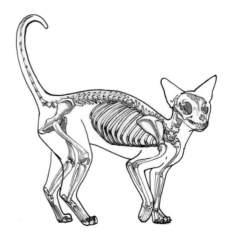

The skeleton. Note the virtual absence of clavicles (collar bones), which enables the forelimbs to encircle a post or tree trunk, and the arrangement of the vertebrae, which allows great flexibility of the spine. In Siamese the caudal (tail) vertebrae are especially slender and easily damaged.

What Is a Siamese?

Siamese Characteristics

To me, all cats are beautiful, but the Siamese hold a special attraction. Part of this attraction comes from their unusual coat pattern and coloring, but the greater part is their personality. Let us look first at the coat, which is much easier to describe than their complex and marvelous personality.

Coat Pattern

The Siamese coat pattern consists of darker coloring on the "points" (face, ears, feet, and tail) and a much lighter tint on the neck and body, producing a dramatic contrast of light and dark.

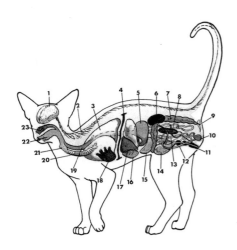

The internal organs.

1. brain	9. anus	16. gall bladder
2. spinal cord	10. testicles	17. liver
3. lung	11. penis	18. heart
4. diaphragm	12. spermatic	19. esophagus
5. stomach	cord	20. trachea
6. kidney	13. small	21. larynx
7. large	intestine	22. mouth cavity
intestine	14. bladder	23. sinus cavities
8. pancreas	15. spleen	

This is called the pointed or Himalayan pattern. Another startling feature of the Siamese is its blue eyes, also a result of the gene responsible for the coat pattern.

Coat Colors

The basic Siamese colors are seal point, chocolate point, blue point, and lilac point. The seal point is the darkest, with the points appearing seal brown to black. The chocolate point has brown points, ranging from bittersweet chocolate brown to pale milk chocolate. The blue point has slate-gray points, and the lilac point, silvery lavender points. In each case the body color should be a very pale tint of the point color. Recently, other point colors have been brought into the Siamese breed by crossing it with domestic shorthair cats. As a result, there are now cats with every imaginable point coloration, including tortie (tortoiseshell) point, red point, and cream point. We will look at the genetics of the various point colors in the chapters on breeding and genetics.

Personality

The Siamese personality is as varied and individual as that of cats in general, but there are some traits that are particularly evident in Siamese. The foremost of these is their loving attachment to their humans. This is the place to confront the terribly wrong idea that Siamese are vicious. I don't know how this bit of misinformation got started, but it was probably the result of improper rearing of kittens, which led to cats that feared and distrusted humans. Siamese kittens, as any others, should have daily, loving contact with people from the moment they are born. The most endearing and common trait of the properly reared Siamese is their attachment to their humans. They want to be, at the very least, in the same room with their person. How close to their person can vary from time to time and cat to cat, but most will seek close contact often, particularly when their person settles in a chair or a bed. Experienced Siamese watchers long ago discovered that there are lap Siamese and shoulder Siamese, a distinction that seems to be hereditary. My first Siamese was a shoulder cat, that being his favorite spot to sit or drape himself even when we walked around, and I still see him in memory perched on my too-patient mother's shoulder and head as she sat at her sewing machine.

Voice

Another special trait of the Siamese personality is their voice and how they use it. The voice itself is very different from non-Siamese breeds; it is usually louder and much more variable in tone and pitch. They have been mistaken for crying babies, but don't let that put you off. That intensity of vocalization will not be prolonged if you are smart enough to understand what dire need must be attended to by you. Most of the time they talk at a conversational level, and many seem to enjoy spoken exchanges with their humans. Their vocabulary can be quite extensive, much beyond mew and meow. As with all generalizations, there are exceptions. We had with us a handsome and exceptionally sweet chocolate-point male, whom we had leased for a couple of years. Although he had an illustrious name, we called him Mou because that's the only word he spoke. No matter what the message—"Scratch my chin, please."; "Feed me!"; "Hello, you beautiful lilac-point girl."—the word was always "mou."

Human Interaction

Siamese will follow you around the house, go for walks with you, if permitted, and play games with you, traits that they share with the dog family. Unlike most dogs, however, they may subject you to a probationary period before giving you their total trust. Observing the rules of Siamese etiquette (see "Understanding Siamese," page 20) will make for a speedy acceptance and a lasting bond of affection.

Intelligence

And last but not least, is their intelligence. They are smart and sensitive, particularly to their humans. They are not dumb, incapable of learning, nor inscrutable, as one often hears, especially in comparison to dogs, pigs, and horses. They are feline, and if a person has no understanding of feline nature, he or she may come to those terribly mistaken conclusions. Part of the joy of living with Siamese is learning from them about feline nature and about their individual personalities, for no two Siamese are identical.

In a Nutshell

So, if the image of a sleek, graceful, blue-eyed, communicative, responsive, and loving feline companion appeals to you, the Siamese is your cat. If you do not already have a Siamese, the first chapter will help you find one.

Acquisition

First Steps

The hardest part about getting your Siamese cat or kitten is patience. It is very hard to resist the temptation to just go out, find a Siamese, and take it home. But think of your long term goal—a long, happy relationship. This calls for thoughtful preparation.

Examine Your Commitment

First, be certain that you are ready, that you understand the responsibilities involved, and that you are prepared to make a commitment to love and care for the cat for its lifetime—which in Siamese may be 20 years. What is "ready"? A young woman once came to me for a kitten. She seemed very mature, financially able, and very eager to share her life with the kitten. She called frequently, both while waiting for the time to pick up her kitten and afterward to tell me how happy she was with it. But before a year passed, she asked me to take back the cat, an adult now, as her new boyfriend was jealous of it. Obviously, this person had not been

ready. (Fortunately, a friend of a friend *was* ready, adopted the cat, and has made a happy and secure home for it ever since).

Self-Test

The following questions will help you decide if you are ready to have a Siamese. If you answer no to three or more questions, there are too many strikes against the likelihood of a long and happy Siamese-person relationship and you should either delay getting a cat or get a different sort of pet.
• Will I be upset by the inevitable wear and tear on my household goods—the scratch on the piano bench, the pulled thread on the sofa, the broken cup?
• If there are other members of the household, do they agree to having a cat?
• If there is a landlord, does he or she allow pets?
• If there are children in the household, will I make certain that they learn how to treat a cat and make sure it is not abused?
• Will my Siamese have companionship (a person or another pet) most of the time?
• Am I willing to stay home weekends until it is adjusted to its new home?
• When I leave the cat for a time, will I be able to get a friend, neighbor, or professional cat-sitter to care for it?
• Can I deal with cleaning up after a sick cat (which is likely to include diarrhea and vomiting), and with nursing it (which may include cleaning wounds and giving medication)?
• Am I aware that kittenhood is very short, and am I looking forward to the adulthood of my Siamese?
• Can I afford the cost of cat food, *not table scraps*, which may be $20 or more per month, and of veterinary care, which may average $200 or more per year?

A queen and kittens at play. This kind of activity is an important component of developing hunting skills.

Acquisition

Kittens and Cats

Another point to remember is that kittenhood is not permanent. As in humans, babies are appealing and very playful, but adults are quieter and may be thought less "cute." Adult Siamese continue to play, but not as much as kittens. Of course, as in humans, adults have more understanding, are more sophisticated, and form deeper and more complex relationships than kittens. If this is not what you want, do not get a Siamese or any other kitten or cat.

A final admonition: Illness will occur even with the best of care. If you would hesitate to take an ailing cat to the veterinarian or would become angry at a cat for throwing up or having diarrhea, please do not get a Siamese or any other cat.

Finding the Right Veterinarian

If you now find yourself ready to begin a long, happy relationship with a Siamese, the next step is to find a suitable veterinarian. Recommendations from friends can be helpful, but there are certain things you should investigate for yourself, as you would in finding a personal physician. The most obvious consideration is location; the veterinarian should be close enough to your home so that travel is not a serious problem. Ideally, the veterinarian's practice is limited to cats, but even in large cities there are few in this category. There are many small-animal veterinarians who treat a sizable number of cats, stay abreast of new findings in feline care, and are aware of the very real physiological differences between cats and dogs. A veterinarian who meets these criteria is a very good candidate for "suitable veterinarian."

If you live in a rural area and only large-animal veterinarians are nearby, do not despair. Just be willing to ask the veterinarian to confer with feline practitioners or to take your Siamese to a veterinary school or major animal hospital for other than routine care. In any case, you should interview prospective veterinarians before getting your Siamese. In the interview try to determine whether the veterinarian will be willing to take time to

explain procedures and conditions to you and whether he or she will be open to suggestions or comments from others, particularly if they do not see many Siamese. After all, you must bear the ultimate responsibility for your pet's health; to make sound decisions for your pet, you need to be an active partner with your veterinarian, not an unquestioning client. The suitable veterinarian will not feel threatened by such an attitude, but will welcome a client who wants to learn and to make informed decisions for the pet.

Finding a Siamese

Sources

Now comes the most exciting part—finding the kitten or cat. Again, you may be fortunate in having leads from friends who have Siamese. If not, check the classified advertisements in newspapers and breeders' advertisements in cat magazines, visit cat shows, and call the major cat registries for breeders in your area (see Useful Literature and Addresses). These sources should yield a first contact with a reputable breeder or dealer. By definition, reputable breeders and dealers are known by and have connections with other breeders and dealers and, if they do not have the Siamese for you, will direct you to others.

Before you contact the breeder or dealer, prepare yourself with a list of questions and be prepared to answer certain questions yourself. You will be seeking assurance that this is indeed a reputable source, and the reputable source will be trying to assess your ability to provide a good home for his or her cherished baby.

Above: These lilac-point kittens, bred at the San-Toi ▶ Cattery by Deanne Johnson and Connie Roberts, show different intensity of eye color. For showing, the darker shades are preferred. The kittens' body language (making themselves small) indicates apprehension.

Below: This seal lynx point kitten already has some tabby markings on the points, most noticeable on its tail.

If you are new to Siamese, you really need the support of someone with many years' experience. The best way to gain such support is by buying a cat or kitten from a knowledgeable individual; therefore, your first questions should ask how much experience the breeder or dealer has and whether continued contact and questions from clients, particularly those with their first Siamese, would be welcomed.

Cost

Pet, Breeder, or Show

Another question, of course, must be about price. Most breeders will have three categories: pet, breeder, and show quality. The pet-quality kitten or cat has one or more traits, such as crossed eyes or a kinked tail, that make it undesirable for breeding and unqualified for showing; this will be the lowest-priced category. A breeder usually stipulates that these cats be altered. If you are not interested in breeding or showing and have no objection yourself to the undesirable trait, include them in your search. Breeder-quality Siamese are showable; that is, they have no traits that would disqualify them, but they are deemed by the breeder as not likely to go far in shows because of less serious flaws, such as ears too small or set too high on the head, eyes too round, tail a bit too short for the length of the body, and so on. Many of this quality are sold as pets with an agreement to alter. Show-quality Siamese will be the most expensive and may be subdivided into "show" and "top show." Show quality should come with a guarantee that the cat has no traits that would

prevent it from achieving championship. Top show kittens conform so closely to the Siamese breed standard that they are likely to achieve top wins in shows and national recognition. Do not expect to buy a top show kitten; they are rarely produced, even by top show parents, and are usually kept by the breeder or are offered at top prices to other established breeders and exhibitors. In fact, a breeder who offers to sell a top show kitten to a newcomer should be very closely scrutinized or probably crossed off the list altogether.

Age

The prices for kittens range from a few hundred dollars for pet quality to thousands of dollars for top show quality, and vary from one area to another. Kittens older than six months and adults usually cost less. A breeder may even have an adult for adoption. Perhaps this is the time to put in a word for considering adults as well as kittens. Adult Siamese are capable of adjusting to new homes at any age, so long as they are properly cared for. This case is typical: A kitten was bought by a woman to be the companion of her invalid husband. The kitten was his constant companion until the man's death, about one year later. The distraught widow could not bear the sight of the cat, who reminded her of her husband, and after several weeks of keeping the cat shut in a room by himself returned the bewildered cat to his breeder. The breeder found a home for the cat with a young couple with small children and dogs. The cat bonded to the new family, despite the many differences in lifestyle from his first and second homes, and lived very happily to an old age.

Condition

Health

You should also ask about the health of the kitten or cat and its line (a breeder's term for forebears), including whether there are any congenital problems or predispositions to conditions

Above: These lilac-point kittens have the sleekness and slender structure desired in show quality Siamese.
Below: This inquisitive young seal point exemplifies the so-called apple-head, which is pet quality. This look is still preferred by many. There are no distinct differences in personality between show and pet quality Siamese.

such as cardiomyopathy. A more tactful approach might be to ask about the longevity of its relatives, particularly of its grandparents and older siblings.

Immunizations

The breeder or dealer should be able to assure you that all of the adults and ready-to-go kittens in his or her care have been vaccinated against rhinotracheitis, feline panleukopenia, and calici virus, the so-called three-in-one vaccination. Some sources also immunize against chlamydia, but it is not given as early as the three-in-one. The adults in the cattery should be immunized against feline leukemia ("feleuk") or have certificates of negative leukemia test results dated within the past three months. Many breeders and dealers do not give leukemia vaccine to the kittens that are to be sold, preferring to leave that to the new owner.

Guarantees

Finally, you should ask about guarantees of health and personality. Of course, no one can make absolute guarantees of anything, but reputable sources will have some arrangement to deal with a buyer's dissatisfaction. Some sources insist that the buyer take the cat or kitten to the buyer's veterinarian immediately for an examination. If there is a personality problem, reputable breeders will give a refund for the return of the Siamese within a certain period of time if it is in good health. Beyond those specifications the breeder may not choose to give a refund, but will surely accept return of the cat or kitten.

The Process of Selection

The Seller's Questions

If you decide to purchase your Siamese from a breeder, he or she will have questions for you. These will be aimed at determining whether you will provide a good home and security for a Siamese. Expect to be asked if you have had a Siamese before; if the answer is no, if you have had other cats before; if so, what became of them; whether you intend to keep the cat indoors; if you want it only as a pet or for breeding and showing; and what you would do if you found that you could no longer keep it.

The First Visit

After this first contact, if both sides are agreeable, you are ready to visit the breeder and see the Siamese. If you are buying a kitten, the chances that there are kittens available and old enough to go are slim. Here is where more patience is called for. Ideally, Siamese kittens should be at least 12 weeks old and have had at least two rounds of three-in-one vaccine before going to a new home. Reasons will be given in a later chapter, but it is basically a matter of weaning time and development of the immune system. Most breeders will allow quiet visitors to see kittens once they are about five or six weeks old. It may be possible to make a deposit and reserve your kitten then, if you wish.

When you visit the cattery or pet shop, look at more than the cats and kittens. The place should be clean, but not like an operating room; there should be no strong odors of uncleaned litter pans or of spoiled food; the water bowls should be full and clean; there should be beds in warm places and toys; and there should be evidence of much human contact.

The Clean Kitten

When you handle the kitten, be alert to signs of flea and ear-mite infestation. Fleas may be seen in the short, light fur of a kitten. If not, ruffle its fur backward along its back and look for small, black flecks; these are flea feces and a sure sign that fleas are around. Look into the ears. Excessive amounts of ear wax, which in cats is normally brown, coating the inside of the ear or clumped in the folds could mean ear-mite infestation. If the ears are clean, but look irritated—redder than the skin elsewhere, for example—or the kitten scratches its ears or shakes its head, it may have just undergone an ear cleaning or treatment for mites.

The Healthy Kitten

Judging the health and condition of the Siamese is very easy if you keep in mind the images of the two extremes—a cat in top condition and one that is ill. The ailing cat or kitten will look like a bundle of misery. Its coat is "open" (not sleek), dull, and unkempt. Instead of lying like a sphinx, it keeps its forefeet back and to the sides of its chest, so that its elbows stick up. Its eyes have partly raised third eyelids or "haws." The eyes and nose may be runny or encrusted. The ill cat may also have a bad odor. When held, it has a slack feeling, and when stretched out, it may be bony along the back and swollen in the belly. The happier image is the healthy Siamese. Its coat is clean, sweet-smelling, shiny, and down flat, giving a painted-on look. (A kitten's coat may be fluffy for a time.) When reclining, it looks at ease and comfortable. It is alert and responsive. Its eyes are bright and clear, with no haws showing. When held, it feels firm and taut, even as a young kitten. When stretched out, its body is tubular (unless it has just had a meal) and firm; individual vertebrae are not felt as you run a hand down the spine.

Personality

Judging the personality of the cat or kitten is really a matter of determining how it was treated from birth and whether you feel an initial attraction to it. If it had close, loving contact with humans from the beginning and weaning was not begun before six weeks, the chances are very high that it will be a loving adult with a healthy Siamese personality. How it responds to you will depend upon how you behave toward it. If you have not had much experience with felines, it would be a good idea to follow the example of the breeder in approaching and making contact with the Siamese. Common

sense tells you that you must not appear threatening or loud; so walk and speak softly and make yourself as small as possible as you approach them. Do not expect young kittens to be very interested in humans; from about four to fourteen weeks it is normal for them to be more interested in playing, especially with each other, than anything else.

The Final Decision

If all is to your liking, expect to visit with the breeder and the cat or kitten for at least an hour. By then, you and the breeder will have asked all the questions, have some knowledge of each other, and can tell whether the Siamese in question should go to you. If the decision is yes, your search is over and your life is about to take on a whole new dimension. If no, keep looking; patience and determination will get you to your Siamese.

Conclusion

Accompaniments to Purchase

When you do find your Siamese and are ready to take it home, the breeder or dealer will give you its health records, including dates and kinds of vaccinations, its pedigree, even if you want it only as a pet, and its registration papers. These last may not be given if you are getting a pet-quality kitten, or they may be given if marked "to be altered." The breeder will probably give you all the advice you can stand about its care and feeding. Some even have printed instructions for new owners! Be sure to exchange telephone numbers and get permission to call back for further advice and consultation, if needed.

Going Home

At last the happy moment has arrived and you are taking your Siamese to its new home, which you have prepared as described in the next chapter.

The First Days Together

The first days together should be planned for well in advance of the day the new kitten or cat arrives. Thorough mental and physical preparations will prevent or ease many problems that are common during the adjustment period.

Mental Preparation

By the time the decision to get a Siamese is made, much of the mental preparation has been done. The idea of sharing space and leisure time with a cat is obvious and usually comes to mind first. Perhaps less obvious is the extent and range of interaction between human and Siamese that is likely to occur. And finally, least obvious, is the realization and acceptance of the responsibility for many years, we hope, of care.

Even with the most careful preparations by all concerned, the move to a new home can be scary for a Siamese. There is no way to predict how the new kitten or cat will react. Even littermates can have quite different personalities and very different responses. Be prepared for anything from the terror-stricken invisible kitten under the sofa to the instantly-at-ease, take-charge Major Cat.

Physical Preparation

The physical things that can be done in advance can be categorized as: 1. household insurance, 2. Siamese insurance, 3. necessities and, 4. luxuries.

Household Insurance

Household insurance begins with moving small, fragile objects out of harm's way. Stand in the middle of each room and gaze around the entire room. Imagine a small, furry creature running, skidding, and jumping on and over every surface, and secure anything that could be endangered. Remember, a kitten has more energy and less muscular control than an adult and has yet to learn how high it cannot jump. The soil of large potted plants should be covered with netting or otherwise made inaccessible to little feet. For a kitten, floor-length lace curtains are magnets, so loop them up or put them away until the little one grows up.

Siamese Insurance

Siamese insurance means making your home safe for your feline companion. Access to dangerous places must be blocked off. For a kitten, this includes narrow openings such as under the stove or alongside the refrigerator. Check the areas where pipes go through walls or floors and seal any gaps. For kittens and cats, windows that are opened must have full-length screens. High-rise balconies should have screen doors. Household cleaning solutions or air fresheners that contain formaldehyde or phenol must be outlawed. Poisonous houseplants must be banished or suspended out of reach (for a partial list of poisonous plants, see page 29.)

The Necessities

The necessities are one or more litter pans, depending upon the size of your home and the youthfulness of your Siamese, a water bowl, and a bed. Litter pans come in a variety of styles. Keep it simple and very accessible to start with—a plain pan several inches deep and big enough to allow the cat or kitten plenty of elbow room. Place the pan where the cat can get to it easily. Do not expect any cat to be happy with a litter pan in the basement of a three-story house. If your new Siamese is a young kitten and your house is a spread-out ranch-style or multi-storied home, provide two or more pans until the kitten reaches adulthood. Later, if you want to try fancier arrangements, such as covered pans, do so after the cat is well adjusted to its new home. Get either the same litter the breeder uses or the basic unscented clay granules and put it in the pan to a depth of about two inches. A slotted scoop completes the toilet setup.

Select a location for the food and water station. It should be out of the way but easy to get to. The water bowl should be of glass or ceramic material intended for such use. Some plastics have been

The First Days Together

Necessities. Beds, litter boxes, food and water dishes, and grooming supplies.

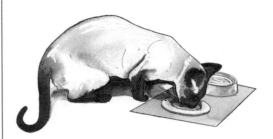

Siamese prefer a regular place for their food and water.

found to be unsuitable water bowls because potentially harmful compounds leach out of the plastic into the water. Dishes for canned food should be flat. Bowls may be used for dry food. An easily cleaned mat of some sort under the food and water dishes is helpful, as some Siamese are messy eaters, either dragging their food out of the dish before eating it or not eating their crunchies over the bowl.

There are all sorts of beds for cats; follow your fancy. The only rules are: 1. they should be appealing to the cat; and 2. they should be washable. To be appealing to the user, they need to be soft and warm. Most Siamese enjoy what I call the doughnut bed. These are simply made and machine washable. Another favorite looks like a wheelless covered wagon in soft sculpture with its top supported with arches of corset stays. Do not be surprised, however, if your special Siamese buddy abandons his bed when you get into yours and wants to share your pillow or to snuggle under the covers by your knees.

Luxuries

Last, but not least, we come to the luxuries—toys, scratching posts, trees, window perches, and the like. (Your Siamese will rank these as necessities, of course). The rule for toys is fun but not dangerous. Examine toys just as you would for human babies. There should be no hard parts that could come off and be swallowed or lodge in the throat. Then, there are special feline dangers. Loose string, yarn, rubber bands, and ribbon can be fatal. While cats can vomit readily, they have great difficulty spitting out long, flexible material, in part because the barbs on the tongue are directed toward the back of the mouth. Once a long, stringy object gets partway down the throat, they cannot rid themselves of it. In the stomach, it may not be bulky enough to cause vomiting and will pass on into the intestine. If these problems are not corrected quickly, a very painful death can result. A friend recently gave my Siamese a mouse made of real fur. It was Ahmin Jhoi's favorite toy until I found that after she dunked it in her water bowl the water turned dark blue. Since she had begun chewing off pieces of the skin and fur, I decided the mouse should be sent to toy heaven. Her little broken heart was mended by a set of sponge balls, a fiber-filled crocheted ball, and a new long, bouncy wire with a heavy brown-paper twist at the end.

Scratching Posts

Some sort of scratching material really is a necessity, not a luxury. One can get by with the simplest sort, such as a scrap of carpet, or get very fancy with scratching posts and cat trees. Again, the

Cat furniture and toys, including scratching posts and a cat tree.

first rule is that of cat-approval. The texture of the carpet should be such that they can really get their claws in and find strong resistance. A low, tight, nubby weave or the jute back of carpeting is very popular among my Siamese. The next consideration is placement. While they are small, a piece of scratching material on the floor is fine. As they get bigger, they want to stretch upward as they scratch. A piece of carpet can be attached directly to the wall or to a board that is set at an angle on a base or around a post set in a base. The height should be slightly more than the cat's greatest reach.

Window Perch

Sitting in windows is a major occupation for Siamese when their people are out of the house. If the windowsills in your home are not wide enough to allow yours to rest and observe the outside world,

a window perch would solve the problem. These are basically carpeted or cloth-covered shelves that are propped on the windowsill.

Cat Tree

The ultimate in luxury is the cat tree, which provides places for scratching, exercise, rest, seclusion, and that most important Siamese duty—supervision of its realm. The tree should be freestanding, not the tension-pole type, and substantial, so that flying leaps do not cause the slightest movement. Cats shy away from things that give way under them. Again, the height is critical. If you want the Siamese on its furniture and not on yours, be sure its tree is taller than your furniture. (A Siamese would lie on a bed of nails if it were the topmost thing around!) At least one company that I know of allows the customer to design the tree, choosing the placement of perches, tunnels, and houses, the overall height, and the color and type of carpeting.

Cat Carrier

Stock up on food and litter, and if you do not already have one, get a cat carrier. A cardboard box with holes punched in it will *not* do. Being enclosed and unable to see out could terrify the cat or kitten, which is bad enough, but a panic-stricken Siamese can tear out of a cardboard box and escape.

Arrival of Your New Siamese

At last the day arrives, and you bring home your Siamese. What you do with it after you get in the front door depends on the state of the cat's nerves and the circumstances in your home. Consider first of all the most reassuring and safest things to do for the cat. At best, whether a cat or kitten, it will be nervous from the trip. Do not be in a hurry to let it out of the carrier. Have the household as quiet as possible. If there are other pets, put them in another room. Everyone should walk and talk quietly. Small children should not be allowed to rush at the cat or

Cat carriers. From top to bottom: A molded plastic carrier of the type suitable for air cargo travel as well as other types of travel. A lightweight carrier of pressed fiberboard suitable for hand carrying. A molded plastic and wire carrier designed to fit under an airline seat.

scream at it, while it is still in the carrier. Whether the Siamese seems calm or nervous, the best idea is to take it to a bedroom or another room that can be closed off before letting it out. One strange room is much less frightening to the Siamese than a whole houseful of new, uncharted territory. An adjoining bathroom could contain its litter box and water bowl. When the Siamese begins to feel at home in the room and with you—it may be in five minutes or three days—introduce it to the rest of the house.

Other Pets

If there are other dogs or other cats already in the home, careful introductions will be needed. Be prepared for the worst—they try to kill each other— and hope for the best—buddies at first sight. First allow the pets to see and smell each other with a barrier between them. This can be achieved by putting the new cat in a cage or its carrier and allowing the older pet to come over and get acquainted. The bars or grill not only prevent fights but give both of them a sense of security. If the first pet is an adult cat and the new Siamese is a kitten, the adult will still probably hiss and swat at the newcomer (in a cat's mind anything new, no matter how small, could be a terrible monster), but will accept it more quickly than if the second cat is also an adult. Do not leave them free in the house together until you are sure there is, at least, a truce. Most do become friends, either immediately or, more usually, after a few weeks.

First Reaction

Even with the smoothest possible transition, the Siamese may not want to eat for the first day or two in its new home. Do not be disturbed unless there are other signs of illness. Put out food and water, of course, and be patient. If you want to try harder, put a dollop of warm, strained baby food chicken or turkey on your finger and offer it to the starveling. If that succeeds, next put a dollop of baby food on top of the regular food.

Adjustment

Whatever the circumstances, the adjustment period will go much faster and more smoothly if the Siamese has maximum contact with its new family. For this reason, most people arrange the homecoming for just before the weekend or a holiday.

As the Siamese begins to move freely around its new home there are bound to be transgressions; after all, it wasn't born knowing that it should not jump on the stove or sit in that chair. Deal with these mistakes very gently until you are sure the Siamese trusts you and will be annoyed, but not frightened, when you raise your voice.

During these first few weeks together you are forming the basis for what can be a true friendship across species lines, a friendship that provides insight into and rewards from a fascinating and loving creature.

The Stages of Siamese Life

Relation to Human Age

A Siamese goes through the same stages of life as a human—although at a quicker pace—and with many of the same characteristics. The Siamese lifespan is much shorter than the human, but a comparison can be made by letting the first year of feline life equal 20 human years and each feline year thereafter, three human years. Thus, a Siamese at three years is roughly the same as a human of 26 years, and Granmaw, a blue point who lived to be 24 years old, was about 90 human years old.

Early Kittenhood

Birth to Three Weeks

Kittenhood lasts from birth to eight months, according to all the cat registries, but growth and development may continue well beyond that time. During early kittenhood one can see all the stages of human child development. For the first two or three weeks the kittens are focused on the mother, nursing and sleeping and receiving her care. Soon thereafter, they begin to react to her and their siblings, patting her on the nose and making the first awkward attempts at play with each other.

Four to Ten Weeks

The next phase of kittenhood, from about four to ten weeks, finds the kittens gaining in motor skills and becoming very active. They are much like human two- to-three-year-olds, into everything and alternating between periods of frenetic activity and total exhaustion. Towards the end of this phase the most precocious ones in a litter begin to seek human attention; this is the beginning of the social-ization phase, which seems to click on somewhere between twelve and fourteen weeks. (In reality, their turning to humans for affection is conditioned by handling from birth; without close contact then they would not later become as trusting of humans).

Late Kittenhood to Puberty

From four to seven months the baby teeth are replaced by the permanent teeth, and by eight months most of the kitten's growth has been attained. Sometime between five and twelve months, puberty usually arrives. Again, the timing is highly variable. Our Stringh Beene, a gentle lilac point who never had an unkind thought, was eighteen months old before he had a clue about sex. At the other extreme are the many tales of unexpected litters sired by six-month-old kittens. Whenever puberty happens, it is hard to miss. When the female goes into her first heat cycle (estrus), she calls loudly and rolls on the floor. The male does not have cycles, but when he is sexually mature his urine will take on a much stronger odor, he may start spraying, which is a way of marking territory and advertising for females, and he may become very restless, particularly at night.

Altering

Unless they are to be bred, the young Siamese should be altered soon after puberty. Otherwise, the female will cycle in and out of heat every other week for up to three months, go out for a few months, and then start all over again. The strongest drive in the adult Siamese male is to mate; if he is kept from it, he will be terribly frustrated.

Young Adulthood to Middle Age

In general, the Siamese is in its physical prime from one to five years. The years from about six to twelve or so can be viewed as middle age, although many Siamese seem not to change at all during this time, except perhaps to put on a little weight. Barring illness, they may remain as playful and active as a four year old.

The Stages of Siamese Life

Advanced Age

The teen years bring the first signs of old age, but not necessarily severe problems. After twelve the Siamese usually slows down a bit, may not look as sleek as it did at five, and should be watched carefully for changes that could indicate disease. At this stage the teeth may start to go, but this is not a serious threat to their health, so long as diseased gums and teeth are treated promptly.

It is not unusual for Siamese to live to be 15 and above. This last stage of Siamese life will see a further gradual decline in activity and an increased concern for the comforts of life—the sunny windowsill should have ample padding for the aging joints and a chair or kitchen step stool nearby to save the effort of jumping that high. If they were fussy about anything before, they will become even fussier in old age, just as we humans do.

The one thing that does not change with age is the love of the Siamese for its people.

Euthanasia

It is in this stage in the life of a Siamese that you are most likely to face a very difficult decision: whether to end its life by euthanasia. Your veterinarian can give you information and advice, but the final decision is yours. My best advice is to watch your cat very carefully. When it seems to you that its discomfort is not counterbalanced by some happiness that day, it is time. Once I waited too long because I was loathe to let my very dear Charlie go; I still regret his last days. But it was a mistake that I have not repeated. Fifteen years later, when his daughter, Tekena, was at the point in her illness where her joy in life was rapidly declining, she was put to sleep. (That phrase is not totally euphemistic, as they do lose consciousness first, just as in natural sleep.) Because of several recent visits to the hospital and the skill and gentleness of her veterinarian, she was not upset by the procedure, which must have seemed to her just another injection.

Understanding Siamese

Feline Nature

Cats are neither inscrutable, mysterious, mystical, nor any of those other fanciful designations that would have you think that feline behavior cannot be understood. What rubbish! Of course, cats (even Siamese) can be understood, but in terms of their nature, not ours. All it takes is understanding the feline nature, the basics of which are extremely simple and can be understood very quickly. Going beyond the basics can be a mutually satisfying occupation for you and your Siamese and one that will provide many years of delightful discovery, for while the basics are simple, what is built on them can be complex and fascinating.

The Predatory Cat

First of all, cats are predators, which means they are hunters. Even without ever having hunted anything ourselves, we know that successful hunting requires keen senses, patience, caution, stealth, quick responses, and the ability to learn.

The Elusive Cat

In the wild, smaller cats are the prey of larger predators. All of the above attributes serve not only to feed them, but to keep them from being food for other predators. These characteristics of cats, then, are doubly important to their existence and have been very strongly set by natural selection. And even though they have lived with humans for 4,000 years, these basic characteristics have not been lost.

The Nocturnal Cat

This is not to say that individuals cannot learn different ways of behaving. For example, cats are nocturnal, hunting mostly at night, yet most pet cats adjust to their human's pattern of activity and sleep at night. A notable exception is the lilac-point gentleman named Willie, who does not sleep through the night and has trained his person to get up before dawn to give him fresh food for his first meal of the day.

Feline etiquette. Top: Asking permission with licks. Bottom: Showing disrespect.

Social Behavior

Cats are social animals. Several studies of groups of cats, both domestic and feral, have shown this, which is quite contrary to the popular idea of the domestic cat as solitary. In cat society there are modes of behavior that serve to minimize fighting and thus the possibility of injury. A major one is the establishment of a dominance-subordinate hierarchy. While this may involve skirmishes and aggressive behavior in the beginning, in the long run there is less fighting because of the recognition and acceptance of positions in the system.

Communication

Communication among members is essential to any society, including feline. Cats communicate with each other through body position, movement, and scent; through facial expression; and by voice. Any one or combinations of these can inform others of a range of intention from challenge to proposal of friendship or more.

Understanding Siamese

The *flehmen* response. Odors are detected by special cells just behind the upper incisors.

Territoriality

Then there is territoriality, an aspect of feline nature that relates to predation and communication. Studies of wild cats show that they have home ranges, which is common among predatory species. As they move about their range, cats leave scent marks along the way. These may be urine containing a special oily substance, which is sprayed onto upright objects from a standing position, or scent from skin glands on the head, tail, and paws, which is transferred to objects as the cat rubs or scratches them. These chemical messages are "read" by others through the vomeronasal gland, which is a small sac of olfactory tissue with openings just behind the upper incisors. In order to get the scent molecules into the gland, the cat lifts its upper lip, opens its mouth slightly, and sniffs; this is called the *flehmen* response.

Mothering

Finally, there is the behavior of mothers toward their kittens. The purring, kneading, and "presenting" (turning the rear toward another) of adults can be traced to the instinctive behavior of young kittens and mothers. There is evidence that the sound of purring by the kittens promotes the release of milk from the mother's glands, as does the repeated pressing with their hands as they nurse. At this stage, the queen grooms the kittens frequently, particularly the perianal region, which results in the evacuation of the urinary bladder and the bowel. The kitten learns that these activities lead to satisfaction and relief, and they become part of its body language as an adult.

Summary

That completes the short list of behavior basics. To understand your Siamese, think in terms of traits related to being
• a hunter and hunted
• nocturnal
• social
• communicative
• territorial
• mothered

Behavior Analysis

Let us apply this basic information to the behavior of Simon, the typical young, altered Siamese in typical home situations.

Olivia, Simon's person, comes home every workday at six. Simon is always waiting at the door to greet her *(KEEN HEARING)* and rubs against her ankles *(MARKING AND CLAIMING AS PART OF HIS TERRITORY)*. He usually talks to her in high-pitched, strident tones *(HI, MOM. I'M GLAD YOU'RE HOME. FEED ME, FEED ME, FEED ME!)*. Olivia understands what Simon is saying and also knows that he has accepted her as a surrogate cat-mother. Being a good Siamese person, she immediately opens a can of Simon's favorite food and puts down a dish of it, giving him a little extra because he's obviously so hungry. Simon wolfs it down *(EAT AS MUCH AS YOU CAN AS FAST AS YOU CAN BEFORE SOMEBODY BIGGER OR FIERCER COMES ALONG.)*, but fills up before he can finish the last bit. He stands over the dish and makes swiping motions on the floor toward it *(GOTTA COVER UP THESE LEFTOVERS BE-*

FORE THE SMELL ATTRACTS SOMEBODY BIGGER OR FIERCER.). Finally satisfied that he has swiped around the dish enough, he saunters into the living room to his favorite chair, going not directly across but around the sides of the room *(THERE'S DANGER IN OPEN SPACES; KEEP TO COVER WHENEVER POSSIBLE.).* After a nap and helping Olivia watch TV, Simon visits his litter box. When he is done, he covers up the soiled litter *(CAN'T GIVE THOSE PREDATORS A CLUE THAT YOU'RE IN THE NEIGHBORHOOD.).*

To a Siamese, cleanliness is way beyond godliness. Some have been known to refuse to enter a dirty box, leaving their deposits on the floor beside the box *(DIRTY FEET, SMELLY TRAIL, AND THE NEXT THING YOU KNOW T. REX IS ON TOP OF YOU!).* In fact, cats can be trained to use the people toilet, particularly if they try to perch on the edge of even a clean litter box, which indicates they do not like the litter under their feet.

Olivia feels sorry for Simon, home by himself all day *(CATS SLEEP ABOUT 18 HOURS A DAY.),* and decides to get him a buddy. She calls his breeder and, sure enough, there is a little brother ready for a new home. Olivia is so pleased to present him to Simon. Simon, however, is something less than pleased by this surprise *(SURPRISES CAN MEAN DANGER.),* hisses, runs away, and hides *(I NEVER SMELLED HIM BEFORE, HOW DO I KNOW WHAT HE MIGHT DO TO ME?).* The new kitten, now named Legree, and Simon gradually make friends as Simon discovers that Legree is really just a little cat and not some small but vicious predator. Soon, Simon is grooming Legree *(SOCIAL BEHAVIOR)* and playing with him *(TEACHING HIM TO HUNT AND FIGHT).*

Eventually, they will become buddies. One, not necessarily the older, will become the dominant one, but very likely they will share dominance, one being top cat in certain places or situations and being subordinate in others. Our Poopsie, Tai Phoon Ta-nuk, our founding queen, was the perfect example. In her middle age she became low cat in the house, but when Poopsie boarded the boat, our summer home, she was immediately, and without dispute, top cat.

Acquired Behavior

Despite all the biological imperatives, the overriding characteristic of the Siamese is its ability to learn. It can learn to trust a human as much as its mother. If its person fosters that trust and affection, the Siamese will become a constant, delightful companion and a source of pleasure all its life and beyond.

The Language of Cats

Knowing some of the language of cats is much more fun than learning a foreign human language. Cat-watching takes on an added dimension. Your Siamese were already pleasing to the eye and the hand, but now you can understand what they are communicating to each other. Better yet, on occasion you can join in the conversation.

Body Language

Much of cat language is expressed by the body. A stiff-legged stance with head and tail extended, staring eyes with contracted pupils, and ears up and turned back is a serious challenge. If the cat's tail bushes and the hair along the spine rises up, stand clear, as it is on the verge of attacking. A cat so enraged has no access to its reason, will not recognize a beloved human or cat buddy, and will attack even a fleeing, submissive cat. Indoors this rarely happens, but the rage center in the brain can be set off by the scent from one male to another and by the threat of one cat to another's young kitten. At the other end of this confrontation range is extreme submissiveness. The ears are flattened out to the sides, the pupils are dilated, and the cat crouches or rolls over, perhaps to protect itself from the feared attack. This is not the time to try to join in the conversation. Do not try to touch them, but put a dustmop, a coat, or a heavy throw rug between them

Understanding Siamese

Total body language. Top, left to right: At ease, friendly mood. Uncertain, slightly apprehensive. Bottom, left to right: Apprehensive. Threatened, frightened.

to break the spell of rage and fear and to separate them.

Body language that sends friendly messages is much more common and certainly more welcome. The friendly face has an open look, the size of the pupils is appropriate to the light level, and the ears are erect and forward. The body is relaxed or the back slightly arched, with the tail up like a flagpole. The ultimate in friendliness is the slow blink. While looking into your eyes, the cat will slowly close and then open its eyes. We don't have tails to signal with, but we can certainly return the slow blink or even initiate a friendly exchange. Even fearful strays will respond if you crouch down (to appear less threatening) and give them repeated slow blinks.

Grooming

Mutual grooming is another expression of friendliness, and one in which humans, armed with a brush or comb, can join, although being washed by the rough tongue of a Siamese can be hard to take, however flattering.

Rules of Etiquette

Cats have etiquette, also. When one cat is in place and a second wants to join it, the polite behavior is for the second cat to approach, give the settled cat two or three licks on the head or neck, and to wait in the standing position. If the response is a return of the licks, that means, "You are welcome to join me." If the response is just calmness, that means, "Okay, but don't crowd me." A mean look, low growl, or more overt displeasure obviously means, "Permission denied."

When cats approach each other, the polite thing to do is touch noses. If they are good friends, they may rub heads and necks. On the other hand, a full stare is an insult. But the biggest insult of all is when one cat sticks its nose right into the body fur of another and then does the *flehmen* response.

Vocal Language

Studies of cat vocalizations describe sixteen different voice patterns. (There may be more distinguishable by cats.) These are classified as murmur patterns, vowel patterns, and strained-intensity sounds. The murmurs include purring and other closed-mouth sounds associated with contentment and friendliness. A queen talking to her kittens uses many of these. The vowel sounds account for most of the conversational vocalizing of the cat, for which the Siamese is justly famous. A multitude of cat words such as meeow, yow, mow, ngow, and mow-wow, indicate greetings, requests, demands, denials, and frustration. The strained-intensity sounds are those used in attack and defense—hisses, growls, and screams—and in mating. The call of a female in heat can sound like a bugle and travel just about as far. The male calls also, and when a female in heat is within range, sings a high-pitched, chirrupy love song. The scream-roar of the female as copulation is completed is unique. Quite different, but also unique, is the chatter, usually elicited by seeing a bird or a squirrel. Dear Phusatti was a great huntress of flies and always chattered and clacked before bringing down her prey.

Nutrition

With cats, as with all living things, good health requires good nutrition. This means not only the right nutrients, but the right proportions of nutrients to each other, and the proper total amount of them.

Feline Nutrients

Nutrients, which are substances that provide nourishment, include proteins and amino acids, carbohydrates, lipids (fats), vitamins, minerals, and even water. These categories are the same both for humans and for other mammals, such as dogs. Because of this, people sometimes think that a cat can be fed a diet of table scraps or dog food. This is wrong! Cats have a metabolism that is quite different in many ways from that of dogs and humans and consequently have dietary requirements that are distinctly feline. The most famous (or infamous) case involved a young cat that was going blind; the veterinarian discovered that its owners were vegetarians and were feeding the cat a vegetarian diet. Happily, further research led to the discovery of the requirement of the amino acid taurine for the maintenance of vision as well as heart function. As the name taurine (Taurus, the bull) indicates, this is not an amino acid that occurs in soybeans and lettuce. Cats are carnivores; they must have animal protein and animal amino acids.

Another important difference between cats and dogs is the cat's much higher requirement for lipids. Some studies indicate that a kitten needs a diet that is 30% or more lipid. Not only do they need more fat than other species, but they must have some animal fat in the diet. Again, plant oils are lipids, but they are different from those produced in animals. A carnivore's metabolism requires animal nutrients. If this presents a problem for strict vegetarians, they should get a pet that is a natural vegetarian, not a cat.

Commercial Foods

While feline nutrition is an entire field of study on its own, we do not have to be experts to provide the proper diet for our Siamese. There are many well-formulated commercial cat foods that are 100% nutritionally complete for cats. These come in both wet (canned) and dry forms. There is a semi-moist form, also, but it contains propylene glycol, which is not listed on the label, and high levels of preservatives. Every veterinarian and feline nutritionist I have heard or spoken to recommends against the semi-moist food.

Dry versus Wet Foods

Until recently there was concern about the safety of feeding dry food to cats because of the possibility of causing urinary problems. For a time, the recommendation was to avoid "high ash content" foods. The ash content of anything is what is left after incineration—the minerals. Obviously, cats must have calcium, phosphorus, potassium, magnesium, and other elements, which provide structural support and cellular function. But since urinary gravel, which can cause bleeding and blockage of the urinary tract (Feline Urinary Syndrome, FUS) and death of the cat, is made of minerals, it was logical to suspect that minerals were at fault. Research in this area was very successful in finding that magnesium was the culprit. Cat-food manufacturers have modified their formulations to lower magnesium content in both wet and dry foods. (Magnesium in small quantities is essential to life, so it cannot be eliminated altogether.) The amount of magnesium is listed on the labels of all the good-quality foods. The general rule is that magnesium should be less than 0.1% of the diet or no more than 230 mg/1000 Kcal. As long as this requirement is met, it does not matter whether the food is wet or dry. Of course, a cat eating dry food will need more water, as canned foods are about 78% water.

Another consideration when choosing between wet and dry foods is convenience. Because of the very low water content of dry food, bacteria cannot grow in it, and it can be left without spoiling. There is some evidence that eating dry food helps keep the teeth clean. Finally, there is the cat's preference.

My Charlie refuses to eat canned food. If I put some down for him, he takes one sniff and proceeds to try to cover it up, swiping the floor all around the dish. The message is very clear. His grandmother, Phussati, also preferred dry food, but lost most of her teeth when she was in her teens. A little water added to her plate of crunchies turned them into mushies, and the problem was solved.

Dyes

One last word about dry food: Avoid those that have coloring added. My Siamese get upset stomachs from the dyes that are added to some dry foods. These dyes are not nutrients; they are put there to please the eye of the purchaser. Choose instead the unappealing (to our eye), uncolored, drab foods that, at least, will not leave permanent orange stains on carpet or upholstery if a starving Siamese eats too much too fast and "upchucks."

Some breeders feed only dry food and others both dry and wet. If you feel confused or uncertain about what to feed, ask your veterinarian and the breeder of your Siamese for recommendations and advice.

Amount and Frequency of Feeding

Once you find good foods that your Siamese likes, the only remaining problem is to resist overfeeding it. Some Siamese have a normal governor on their appetites, but others eat like starvation is just around the corner. Your veterinarian can measure the height of your cat and give you its optimum weight. In general, Siamese females in good shape are five to seven pounds, and the males, eight to ten pounds, depending on the size of their bone structure.

Guide to Feeding

The best guide to how much to feed your cat is the cat's appearance. The Siamese in good trim should have a tubular body, not a fat or saggy one. It should not be so thin that there are hollows in front of its hips. When you run the palm of your hand down its back, you should not feel individual vertebrae. Once your Siamese is in good shape, note its weight for future reference. (Your veterinarian has small animal scales, or you can stand on your own bathroom scales while holding the cat, note the combined weight, then release the cat and subtract your weight.)

Schedules

A twice-a-day feeding schedule is usual for adults, although some feed only once and others three times. A bowl of water should be available at all times.

Kittens and young cats up to the time when full growth is attained need to be fed more freely and more frequently. At this stage it is better to err on the side of excess food than not enough.

Females in the second half of pregnancy and lactating females should have as much food as they want, as should all cats that are recuperating from surgery or an illness.

As your cat ages, it becomes less active and needs fewer calories to maintain its optimum weight. There are several commercial cat foods that are formulated with fewer calories for the less active cat.

The watchword is vigilance. The owner must be mindful of the cat's condition and adjust its diet to suit its changing needs.

Environmental Hazards

The outdoor environment is so filled with hazards that no Siamese should ever be put outside. The thought of speeding traffic, wild predators, malicious people, dogs, poisons, disease, and parasites should be enough to prompt any Siamese owner to keep it indoors.

Ingestible Hazards

The indoor environment, while infinitely safer, still may have hazards for the Siamese. Chief among these are things that can be ingested. Siamese are noted for a healthy appetite and superabundant curiosity. This means that many things other than food get put into their little mouths. These ingestible dangers may be categorized as mechanical or chemical.

Mechanical Hazards

Mechanical hazards include small objects that could choke the cat or those that could pierce or block the digestive tract. These include toys that have small metal or plastic parts that can be detached and loose buttons and coins. Loose bits of string or twine can cause obstruction or strangulation of the bowel. Do not leave a sewing basket or pin cushion around the house. Not only is thread fun (and dangerous) to play with, but pins and needles are also attractive, especially needles that are threaded. The cat begins by biting the thread, which gets tangled on its rough tongue, and ends up swallowing thread and needle.

The most dangerous single category is bone. Small bones can choke, pierce the digestive tract, and cause blockage. Everyone knows that a cat should not be given any bone that it could possibly crack with its teeth or swallow. Everyone also knows that there is nothing any cat likes better than chewing on a chicken bone. Do not be tempted to indulge them in this. Poultry bones are notorious for splintering as they break; the sharp, pointed ends can be driven through the wall of the intestine by its contractions or lodge crosswise and obstruct the bowel. Either case is obviously life-threatening. Wimpy, the first born of my first breeding, almost killed himself by opening a closed garbage can and eating chicken bones. Surgery was required to remove the bones from his intestine, complications set in that required further abdominal surgery, and the stress of all that precipitated urinary blockage, which ultimately required more surgery. There was a happy ending to this story, for the Wimp lived to be 19½ years old, but there had been months and months of suffering, large veterinary bills, and untold worry. His owner never again put chicken bones in the kitchen garbage pail. The moral of this story is never trust poultry bones to any container that your Siamese could possible open or knock over. Stash the bones in the refrigerator until they can be taken out of the house. Should your Siamese outsmart you and get at some bones, call your veterinarian at once for advice.

Chemical Hazards

The ingestible chemical hazards are poisons. The problem here is not so much the widely known poisons, such as lye and antifreeze, but the ones we accept as nonhazardous that are poisonous to cats. A very popular household disinfectant contains phenol. This compound and its relatives (look for the word phenol within longer chemical compound names) are not only toxic to cats but accumulate in their tissues over time. This means that whenever Sammi walks over the bathroom floor that has been cleaned with XYZ, the residual phenol is picked up by her feet, which are washed by her tongue, and the poison builds up in her system. Eventually a level

Above: This alert adolescent shows the slight body shading ▶ that is typical of the seal points.
Below: San-Toi's Bently, Jr., bred and owned by Deanne Johnson and Connie Roberts, shows the long triangular head of the show Siamese.

will be reached that causes damage to her liver, kidneys, and other organs. Read the labels of your cleaning solutions and household disinfectants. The best plan is to throw out the cat poisons and instead use a chlorine bleach solution (1 part bleach to 32 parts water), which kills all pathogens (disease-causing microorganisms), leaves no residue, is readily available, and cheap.

Do not be tempted to give any human or canine medication to a cat, unless it is prescribed by your veterinarian. Our common headache and fever remedies, aspirin and acetaminophen, are poisonous to cats. Feline metabolism is very different from ours and other omnivores; they lack the enzymes that other species have that break down certain compounds before they can reach a toxic level.

A complete list of poisons would go on for pages and probably be skipped over by many readers. Instead, consider the following as guidelines (with a few examples) to identifying other household poisons:
• anything with a label that includes "Keep out of the reach of children"
• anything that is intended to kill other organisms (insecticides, fungicides, pesticides, herbicides, mothballs, rat poison, slug bait)
• preservatives and disinfectants (wood preservative, formaldehyde, phenol)
• strong acids (muriatic, battery) and strong alkalis (drain cleaners, oven cleaners, permanent-wave solution, paint remover)

Above left: This youngster shows the paler body color that is typical of the chocolate point.
Above right: This blue point shows a nice alignment of oval eyes and large ears.
Below left: Master Grand Champion Angkor Rose Geronimo of Velvet Paws, a chocolate point bred by Betty White and owned by Joyce Gutches, shows a perfect profile and exceptional muscle tone, in addition to excellent color matching of his points.
Below right: This lilac point has a very fine body matched in length by a whippy tail. Her ears, although of nice size, do not quite follow the line of her cheeks.

• strong oxidants (undiluted bleach, peroxide)
• organic (fat-dissolving) solvents (dry-cleaning fluids, gasoline, home-heating oil, kerosene, turpentine, nail-polish remover, paint thinners)
• paints and polishes
• alcohols, particularly methanol and ethylene glycol (antifreeze, rubbing alcohol, windshield-washer fluid)

Other ingestible chemical hazards are more subtly and enticingly packaged in certain plants, including a number of popular houseplants. Among these poisonous plants are azaleas, caladiums, common or cherry laurel, dumb cane (*Dieffenbachia*), ivies, mistletoe, oleander, philodendrons, and rhododendrons. Poinsettia has long been thought to be poisonous, but recent evidence indicates it may not be. However, when in doubt, avoid risk. Since no cat can resist at least biting a dangling leaf at eye level (and eye level to a Siamese is anywhere it can get to), the safest plan is to banish all poisonous houseplants, cut flowers, and greenery, even dried, from your home. If this is not acceptable, put the plants in a separate room or hang them out of Siamese reach.

Inhalant Poisons

There are also inhalant poisons, which include the fumes of poisonous compounds and many gases. One of these is carbon monoxide, which is produced by gasoline engines. An automobile engine should not be run in a closed garage, even if there are no people or pets in the garage. The fumes can seep into the house undetected, as carbon monoxide is colorless and odorless. Smoke, of course, which can suffocate at high densities, in injurious even in small amounts. Gas stoves and other gas appliances should be checked for leaks. If the house must be fumigated, take all pets out of the house until it is safe for them to return. Any household job that produces irritating or noxious fumes should be done only with good ventilation. On the other hand, if lawns, trees, or crops are being sprayed nearby, be sure to close all windows and doors until the fumes are gone.

Other Hazards

Electrical: Electrical cords are a serious hazard if the Siamese tries to chew on them. They are especially attractive to kittens. Hide all cords, or put them out of reach. If your Siamese is a wire chewer, unplug the cords in the room in which it is left alone. Less common, but just as serious, is the electrical outlet or receptacle. Spraying males have been known to use an open receptacle as a target, resulting in a severe burn to the genitals, not to mention damage to the receptacle and the danger of an electrical fire. Open receptacles should be closed with the small caps designed to protect children from shock.

Drowning: There is not much danger of an adult Siamese drowning indoors, unless you have an indoor pool or are careless about what is in the washing machine when you start it up, but kittens have been known to drown in toilet bowls. So, if you have a young Siamese, keep the lid down and do not leave filled bathtubs unattended.

Sunburn: Siamese are very susceptible to sunburn wherever the fur is short, thin, or missing. These conditions are found on the ears, where the fur is very short; on the face between the eyes and the ears, where the fur is very sparse; and at lesions, where the fur has fallen out. Although cats love to lie in a spot of sunshine, they should not be allowed for extended periods in direct, overhead, unfiltered sunlight.

Miscellaneous: There are many miscellaneous hazards in any household. Open fireplaces, even cold, are dangerous, as cats may be tempted to explore the chimney. Household appliances of all sorts can be hazards. I never close the refrigerator door without checking for Siamese tails in the way. Beware of the possibility of closing your cat in a washing machine, dishwasher, clothes dryer, or cold oven. Hot stoves and ovens, space heaters, any open flame, and electric fans are obvious dangers.

Collars: Cat collars are my final hazard item. Flea collars have been known to cause skin irritation and loss of hair. I see no reason for an indoor cat to have any kind of collar, but if you must put one on your Siamese, be certain that it is properly adjusted, preferably the type that will give way under the weight of the cat, and has no bell. Wearing a bell has been linked to stomach ulcers in cats, and too-loose collars can cause death by hanging or choking if the collar snags on some projection. I have read of cats dying from getting their lower jaw caught under a collar. The collar should be adjusted so that you can fit just one finger under it without causing the cat discomfort, but no looser.

Health Care

Vaccinations

Vaccines were first made from viruses, but now include preparations of parts of viral coats, attenuated or killed bacteria, and other pathogenic microorganisms. When a vaccine is put into a cat, it challenges the cat's immune system, which then multiplies the white blood cells that can neutralize the pathogen represented by the vaccine. Some of these cells are maintained on reserve, so to speak, for months and are called memory cells. Should the cat be exposed to that pathogen, the memory cells are ready to mount an attack against the invaders. To keep up an effective level of memory cells, yearly revaccinations (boosters) are needed in most cases.

The Three-in-One Vaccination

If the Siamese you get is a kitten, it should already have at least one round of at least three vaccines—the so-called three-in-one: *feline panleukopenia, caliciviruses,* and *rhinotracheitis.* Panleukopenia is also known as feline distemper or enteritis and is caused by a virus that can reproduce only in rapidly dividing cells. In newborn kittens this would include nearly every tissue in their bodies. In older kittens and cats the digestive tract is the site of infection, thus enteritis. The family of caliciviruses infect the membranes of the mouth, nose, and throat, causing inflammation and ulcers. They can also produce pneumonia and infect the conjunctiva of the eye. Rhinotracheitis is an upper respiratory infection (URI), a head cold.

Chlamydia

An additional vaccine, against chlamydia, is sometimes included with the three above, making it a four-in-one. Chlamydia is a bacterium that infects the conjunctiva of the eye and the nasal epithelium producing the disease known as pneumonitis. At least two immunizations against these four diseases are needed to begin with, followed by a booster every year.

Leukemia

There is a vaccine against feline leukemia, which is caused by a virus (FeLV). Most breeders and others whose cats go out to shows or to other catteries immunize their Siamese against this disease. This is one of the vaccines that is made from only a part of the virus coat and therefore cannot possibly cause the disease it is designed to prevent.

Rabies

There is no real danger of a strictly indoor cat contracting rabies; however, some state laws allow the confiscation of any cat that is reported to have scratched or bitten someone. This could mean the destruction of the cat in order to determine whether it had been rabid. For this reason alone, it is recommended that rabies vaccine be given to indoor Siamese. If you allow your cat to go outdoors, it should certainly be immunized against rabies.

Feline Infectious Peritonitis

The newest feline vaccine is against one of the deadliest infectious diseases of cats—feline infectious peritonitis (FIP). It is given in nasal drops. Although the majority of cats exposed to this family of corona viruses do not develop the disease, it is highly advisable to have your cat immunized against it, as there is no cure.

Minor Problems and Illnesses

The serious infectious diseases of cats can be avoided or minimized by immunizations. Even so, there will fall into the life of every Siamese a certain amount of minor problems and illnesses. Stomach upsets, head colds, and skin problems top the list. (Sounds very human, doesn't it?) If the minor stomach upset is the result of eating too much, the wrong thing (short of poisonous substances), or too fast, there is nothing to worry about. Cats vomit very easily. The only remaining problem is getting the spot out of the carpet if you use food containing dyes.

Health Care

Upper Respiratory Infections

Although there are few antiviral medications, the cat with symptoms of a head cold—runny eyes, runny nose, sneezes—should be taken to its veterinarian, who may want to prescribe antibiotics to prevent or combat secondary infections. If the head cold, upper respiratory infection (URI), turns out to be feline viral rhinotracheitis (FVR) or "cat flu," it is not a minor illness. The disease is caused by a feline herpes virus that infects the upper respiratory passageways and the eyes. Viruses that infect the nasal membranes are not so dangerous in themselves, but they can cause a serious problem if the cat's nose is so stuffed up that it cannot smell. If the cat cannot smell its food, it will not eat. This can lead to a general downward spiral, with the cat becoming physiologically depressed. If the infection lasts for several days, the cat must be force-fed by putting food or a dietary supplement into the front of its mouth or on its lips. If it stops drinking, water will have to be given by a dropper at home or under the skin at the veterinary clinic.

Skin Problems

Most people think of skin problems as insignificant. While the majority of skin diseases are not life-threatening, they should not be neglected. If your Siamese develops a skin lesion, take it to the veterinarian. It could be something as minor as a fungal infection, which is usually self-limiting, but it also could be a condition that will worsen if untreated or, more importantly, may be a symptom of an internal problem. At the very least, consider that these conditions are unsightly and probably very uncomfortable for the cat.

Most skin lesions are caused by fungus or allergies. The fungal infection commonly called ringworm is one of the few diseases that can be transmitted from cat to human and human to cat. Fungal spores are everywhere, and ringworm can break out with no known contact with another infected person or cat. Fortunately, in most cases—cat and human—it cures itself within six or seven weeks. Even so, it is not advisable to leave it untreated because of the possibility that it will become chronic and that it could be passed to others. It is first noticed when a patch of hair thins or falls out, but the infection has been underway for some time before this happens. As the fungus grows outward, the newly infected skin forms a reddened ring around the older, central part of the lesion, which is usually paler and scaly. There are many antifungal agents that can be used on cats. Your veterinarian should see the cat as soon as possible, make the diagnosis, and prescribe the treatment.

The lesions caused by allergies may at first look like a fungus infection, but they are usually redder in the center than ringworm and may have a more irregular outline. Again, this is something that must be diagnosed and treated by a veterinarian. Cats can develop allergies to foods, parasites, and inhalants that will cause dermatitis. If food allergy is suspected, the veterinarian may recommend an elimination diet—taking away one type of food at a time—or a diet of food that the cat has never been exposed to before, such as lamb. (For allergies to develop there must have been an earlier exposure to the substance, the allergen.)

If fleas have been around, your Siamese could develop flea-allergy dermatitis, which is the most common allergic skin disease in cats. There are several forms in which it may appear, including excessive grooming to the point of wearing the hair down to a stubble, red and elevated hairless areas on the abdomen or back of the hind legs, and a few to hundreds of tiny, crusty bumps either over the entire body or mostly on the head, back, and base of the tail. Obviously, if your Siamese has flea-allergy dermatitis, the fleas have to go. Your veterinarian will be able to advise you on the safest means of banishing fleas and may also want to treat your cat with corticosteroids to give immediate, but temporary, relief.

Allergic-inhalant dermatitis is much less common than flea-allergy dermatitis and food allergies, but produces much the same symptoms. Pollens are the culprits here and strangely enough do not usually produce respiratory symptoms with the dermatitis.

Siamese especially are prone to a condition of the chin skin commonly known as chin acne. The hair follicles become clogged, bacteria grow, and the area looks dirty because of the resultant black particles. The chin is one of the most difficult places for the cat to groom. It does so by washing its paw as it holds it near the chin. A less than thorough cleansing allows bacteria to multiply. Keeping food off the chin is the first order of business; feed wet food in flat dishes, not bowls. If your cat gets chin acne, scrub the skin daily with soap and water, rinse well, and dry with a tissue or paper towel.

A skin problem usually confined to whole (unaltered) adult males is stud tail. An accumulation of a waxy secretion at the upper surface of the base of the tail can produce clogged pores and loss of hair. If not cleaned, the skin may become inflamed and infected. At the first signs—stiff, sticky hair—treat as recommended for chin acne: clean, rinse, and

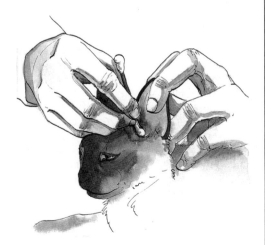

Ear cleaning. Excess wax can be carefully removed with cotton swabs.

dry. Once the skin becomes infected, it is very hard to clear up.

Ear mites are microscopic arthropods that affect the skin of the external ear, living off the cerumen (ear wax) and irritating the skin. The irritation causes an increase in production of cerumen; the ears become inflamed and clotted with excess cerumen. An ear-mite infestation should not be neglected. The mites torment the cat with itching, so that it shakes its head and scratches at its ears: if left untreated, this can lead to hematomas in the ear. The hematomas can cause permanent damage to the delicate cartilage of the external ear, resulting in a crumpled, squashed ear. Buy stock in cotton swabs, use them liberally to clean the ears, and then put mineral oil into the ear canal as you hold the cat's head sideways and massage the base of the ear. The oil suffocates the mites. This treatment may have to be repeated several times over a two- to three-week period. There is also an injectable miticide, but it is not yet approved for use in cats.

Eye Problems

Conjunctivitis, inflammation of the membrane that lines the eyelids and the exposed surface of the eye, can be caused by any number of irritants, mechanical and chemical, allergens, and pathogens and is usually a minor problem, with the exception of the last-mentioned cause. Again, minor does not mean that the problem can be ignored. The susceptibility of Siamese to eye irritations seems more pronounced in the lilac points, perhaps because of their higher degree of albinism. Tekena, a lilac-point female who was shown in the seventies, never went to a show without her bottle of feline eyewash because of the heavy pall of cigarette smoke in the show halls. Even with frequent eyewashes, her lids became red and the third eyelid, the nictitating membrane, extended. Fortunately, with fewer smokers among the exhibitors and smoking banned in most show halls, this is no longer a problem for show Siamese.

Irritations such as those caused by smoke or allergens usually disappear with the removal of the offending substance from the environment of the Siamese. However, the condition can become chronic, especially if it is allowed to persist without an attempt at relieving the situation right away. The main problem with this is not the unsightliness of goopy eyes, nor the discomfort the cat may be enduring, but the possibility of infections developing in this compromised tissue. Infections may lead to swelling of the conjunctiva, elevation of the third eyelid, a yellowish discharge, and sensitivity to light, which causes the cat to squint. If not treated, the infection may produce a cloudiness over the eye. An infection this advanced can cause a corneal ulcer (keratitis), which, if not treated, can become a hole in the eye. The fluid inside the eye, which helps give the eyeball its shape, can escape and pathogens can enter the interior of the eye. At this point, matters become very serious, with the partial loss of vision or the loss of the whole eye distinct possibilities.

Conjunctivitis may also be an early sign of feline viral rhinotracheitis (FVR), discussed above. Whatever the cause, red, runny eyes should not be neglected. The chances are very high that the conjunctivitis will be minor, lasting just a few days and leaving no permanent damage, but increase the chances of a happy outcome by taking your Siamese to the veterinarian promptly and following her or his directions faithfully.

Even with veterinary attention and prescribed medication, eye infections can worsen. One of the reasons is that the medication is rapidly washed out of the eye by tears and must be replaced every few hours. Well, if you've never put medicine in the sore eyes of a Siamese, you have a real treat in store. Siamese can turn themselves into pretzels, back off the edge of tables while their neck skin is in a viselike grip, and generally go berserk when faced with eyedrops or ointment. My most successful method of doing it alone sounds difficult but really is not. Kneel on the floor and sit back on your heels.

Conjunctivitis causes the third eyelids (haws) to elevate instead of retracting into the inner corner of the eyes.

Wedge the patient's body, with its head facing forward (away from you), between your knees. One hand can be used to tilt the cat's head up slightly and, if the cat is struggling to escape, grip the neck skin between palm and last two fingers. The other hand is free to administer the medication. If the medication is in liquid form, just hold the bottle above the eye and let the drops fall in. If it is an ointment, squeeze a small amount onto the thumb side of your index finger and, with a rolling motion, deliver the ointment into the trough between the eye and the lower lid. (You may have to pull the lower lid down a bit with the index finger of the other hand.) Of course, if there are two or three people to help, it is much easier. Joking aside, not medicating frequently enough is a great temptation, especially when Sammi hides when she hears the cap come off the tube and regards you with tearful, hurt eyes afterward. Think of the possibilities of a prolonged infection, which could lead to chronic conjunctivitis, or a more serious infection, which could require months of treatment, much of it at your hands, and stick to the medication schedule.

Applying eye medication. This position leaves the hands free to control the head position and to put the drops or ointment into the trough between the eye and the lower lid.

Internal Parasites

Internal parasites of cats consist mostly of worms. There are feline heartworms, eyeworms, and lungworms, but these are rare compared to the worms of the digestive tract. The intestinal parasites in cats are usually roundworms and flatworms. Several species of roundworms (nematodes) can infest cats, including ascarids, hookworm, and whipworm, with ascarids being the most common. Roundworms have complex life cycles that may involve more than one host animal. The adults lie in the intestine and absorb nutrients from the cat's food or tap into small intestinal arteries. They lay eggs, which pass out with the feces. In some species, the eggs are ingested by and develop in other animals, such as rodents and insects. A cat can become infected by eating an infected mouse or beetle. In other species, the eggs, which can survive for years, are ingested by the cat without an intermediate host. The eggs develop into larvae that migrate through the lungs of the cat, causing a cough or even pneumonia. The larvae can also be passed to kittens through the milk of an infected queen. Infestation is more serious for kittens than adults, but in both may cause vomiting

and diarrhea. Sometimes, roundworms can be seen in the vomit or feces. Fortunately, they can be eliminated from cats by careful hygiene, keeping the cat from walking on grass and soil, preventing it from capturing and eating prey, making sure that it eats only cooked meats, and having a veterinarian prescribe a course of treatment.

Flat worms include tapeworms and flukes. Flukes, which can infest lungs, liver, and intestines, are rare in housecats and usually are gotten from eating raw fish. Much more common in cats are tapeworms, which lie in the intestine—to which they attach by one end, the scolex—and soak up the digested food. Segments (proglottids) are continually produced from the region just behind the scolex, forming a long ribbon. At the other end of the ribbon, the segments, which are loaded with fertilized eggs, break off and make their way out of the cat's anus. At this stage they look like grains of cooked rice and may creep about, carrying what are now embryos. The proglottid dies and disintegrates; the embryos are eaten by flea and lice larvae,

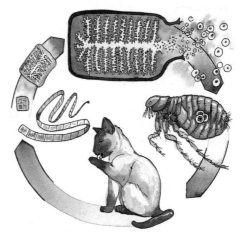

The tapeworm life cycle. The flea carries the microscopic larvae, which can be transmitted to the cat by a flea bite. The larvae migrate to the intestine and develop into a flat strand of segments, which absorbs nutrients from the contents of the intestine.

which can then pass them on to their hosts. If you find a flea on your Siamese, wait two or three weeks to give the tapeworm larvae time to get to the digestive tract, and then have your veterinarian give it a Droncit tablet or injection. Before Droncit was discovered, tapeworm treatment consisted of a substance that caused intestinal contractions that were painful to the cat and usually left the scolex in place. Droncit affects the cuticle of the tapeworm, the outer covering that normally protects it from the cat's digestive juices, and the whole worm is digested. This compound is very effective and need be given only once, unless Sammi picks up another flea.

The final caution about minor problems and diseases is that they have the potential to become major and should never be neglected.

Potentially Serious Symptoms

This section could be entitled "When to Call the Veterinarian," but I have already advised you to call the veterinarian whenever anything looks amiss. The following are symptoms that absolutely cannot be ignored, although some of them may not necessarily indicate a serious illness.
- bleeding, from a wound or any body opening
- difficulty in breathing, usually with the neck extended and mouth open
- repeated vomiting and/or diarrhea
- refusal to eat and drink
- extreme lassitude and nonresponsiveness
- seizures
- pupils unresponsive to light or different from each other
- inability to maintain normal posture
- lameness or inability to walk normally
- signs of disorientation, such as walking in circles or bumping into objects
- difficulty in giving birth
- difficulty in urinating or urinating outside the litter box
- unexpected weight loss

- increase in fluid intake and output (urine)
- lumps and swellings, particularly of the abdomen
- abdominal tenderness
- persistent cough, wet or dry
- a general appearance of illness—uncomfortable looking, coat open, elbows up, distant gaze

The implications of these various symptoms are too many to describe here. Some are quite obvious. All of them should be taken very seriously, and the occurrence of any one of them should result in an immediate call to your veterinarian.

Health and condition. The healthy Siamese is sleek and smooth, neither bony nor flabby. The sick Siamese may have an "open" coat, loose skin, and look very uncomfortable. The very ill Siamese often lies in an elbows-up position.

Genetics

Introduction

The idea of breeding Siamese is attractive to most, but not many want to learn about Siamese genetics. It should be the other way around. Breeding can be very costly in time, effort, emotion, and money, and should be undertaken only after careful consideration of the difficulties involved and with a full commitment to the project. The basics of Siamese genetics, on the other hand, are not difficult to understand and can be lots of fun. Let's start with genetics and work through to the more difficult subject: breeding.

Basic Coat-Color Pattern

Coat color and pattern in the Siamese cat are the result of the interaction of several different genes and the environment. At first glance this seems impossibly complex, but if we consider one kind of gene at a time, most of these difficulties disappear. Before we tackle specific genes, let us establish a few working definitions and briefly review how genes function and are inherited.

Definitions

Inheritance: Just as in humans, cats inherit one set of chromosomes from each parent through the fusion of an egg cell, which has one of each kind of chromosome from the mother, and a sperm cell, which has one of each kind from the father. (The common term for this process is fertilization, but fusion of the two cells is what really happens.) The new individual thus has a double set of chromosomes, as did its parents. These chromosomes provide for its development as a cat instead of a rat, as well as its individual inherited characteristics, such as eye color, coat length, and coat color. In the developing embryo some cells will be set aside to become *gametes* (sperm or eggs); geneticists and embryologists call these the *germ line*. The remainder and greater part of the embryo will provide for the development of all the rest of the individual; those cells are called the *somatic (body) line*. Muta-tions that occur in the somatic cells—the skin, the liver, or the blood, for example—cannot be passed on to the next generation. Only those cells of the germ line that develop into gametes and participate in a fusion can carry genes, mutated or otherwise, from the parents to the offspring.

Gene: A gene is a linear portion of the DNA of a chromosome that is responsible for the way a certain cell product is put together by the cell's metabolic machinery. Since all the cells of an individual, with the exception of its gametes, have a double set of chromosomes, all of these cells have two of each kind of gene (or multiples of two, if a particular gene exists as more than one copy per single set of chromosomes).

The DNA of a gene itself doesn't do anything; DNA is a passive molecule, lying in the nucleus of the cell and serving as a template for the construction of similar, but shorter, molecules: RNAs. It's the RNAs that do all the work of the gene. It's as though the DNA sits in the nucleus, the inner sanctum of the cell, and tells the RNA to go out into the cytoplasm, the workshop of the cell, and put together a string of amino acids in a certain linear order, forming a protein. This protein may be a regulatory protein, such as a hormone; it may be a structural protein, supporting some part of a cell; or it may be an enzyme, a "shaker and mover" protein, all depending on what gene was responsible for its synthesis.

Now comes the wonderful, complicating factor that provides for that "spice of life"—variety! A gene may undergo a change such that it becomes different enough from the original form of the gene to make a detectable difference in its cell product. If this happens in a gamete that participates in fusion, the resulting offspring will carry that genetic change, which is a *mutation*, and may show the effect of the altered cell product. The original form of the gene is called the *wildtype* and the new form is the *mutant*. Additional mutations can produce even more different forms of that one gene. All the different forms of a gene are called its *alleles*.

Genetics

Homozygosity: When both copies of a certain gene are identical in information, that is, they consist of the same allele, we say that the individual is homozygous for whatever trait is governed by that gene.

Heterozygosity: This term describes the situation in which an individual has two different alleles for a certain gene. The result of being heterozygous for a certain gene will depend upon the kind of cell product governed by that gene and the kind of changes that produced the different alleles. In some instances, each allele will provide for the synthesis of its variant cell product so that there will be both variant products in the heterozygous cell (and thus in the individual). This relationship between two alleles is called *nondominance* or *codominance*. In other instances, the effect of one allele masks the effect of the second allele; this relationship is called *dominance/recessiveness*. The allele that expresses itself even when present in only one copy is the "dominant" one; the other allele's expression will not be evident unless the individual is homozygous for this "recessive" allele.

Now, let us go back for a closer look at the gene product, the proteins. The most important type of product for an understanding of Siamese colors and pattern is a class of proteins called *enzymes*.

Enzyme: An enzyme is a protein that functions as a chemical catalyst. All proteins start out as a long string of amino acids. Which amino acids are strung together and in what order is specified by the messenger RNA that is made off the DNA of the gene for that protein. Proteins that are enzymes usually fold up into a more or less globular shape. Each enzyme has a particular three-dimensional shape, which is the result of its unique sequence of amino acids. This three-dimensional shape is critical to its ability to act as a catalyst. Anything that causes a change in the shape can affect the enzyme's effectiveness.

Metabolic Pathway: This pathway is the sequence of chemical changes that are required for the synthesis, alteration, or breakdown of molecules in cells. Think of these pathways as assembly lines where larger molecules (such as pigments) are made from smaller subunits, as detail shops where parts of molecules can be altered, and as disassembly lines where molecules are taken apart into their subunits.

Often, metabolic pathways are depicted as diagrams. These diagrams may be oversimplified, but they do allow us to see at a glance how the metabolic machinery works.

enzyme #1   enzyme #2   enzyme #3

$$A \longrightarrow B \longrightarrow C \longrightarrow D$$

A is the starting molecule or precursor, each arrow is a chemical change, and above each arrow is the specific enzyme needed to catalyze that step, to effect that chemical change. Different kinds of enzymes are required for each step in a metabolic pathway. The enzyme itself is unchanged and can catalyze its particular step repeatedly. B and C are intermediates in the pathway to D, the end product. Each step depends on the one to its left. If B is not formed, neither C nor D can be made, even if enzymes #2 and #3 are present and in working order. Once all of the steps of a pathway are accomplished, the end product (D) has been made. If D is the pigment melanin, the hair growing from cells that have this metabolic pathway will be pigmented.

Hair Formation

That brings us to the formation of hair. You may remember that classic diagram in all biology textbooks—a cube of skin with a hair projecting from its follicle. At the bottom of the follicle is the hair root, and at the very bottom center of the root is a small bulb of connective tissue and capillaries, the papilla. Over the papilla is the layer of cells that actually produce the hair. These cells grow and divide, pushing upward as they form the shaft of the hair. They also produce pigment if genes and environmental conditions permit. Not long after the cells are pushed upward by the new cells forming below them, the cells of the hair shaft die, but maintain their integrity and attachments to each other. The part of the hair that is seen projecting from the skin is composed of dead cells that still contain certain molecules, such as keratin and pigments, which were made when the cells were alive. One more thing to remember about hair—it stops growing after a time and falls out. How long the papilla cells will remain active and continue to lengthen the hair shaft is under the control of the nervous and endocrine systems and can be affected by the environment.

Restriction of Color

Now, let us relate all of this to the basic coat pattern of the Siamese with its acromelanism, the restriction of color to the extremities. The explanation for this strange pattern is actually very simple: a mutation occurred in one of the genes that provide for the various enzymes needed for the production of pigment. The mutation resulted in an enzyme that was less firmly held together in its three-dimensional shape than the wildtype enzyme; because of this, when the mutant enzyme is subjected to temperatures of approximately 98°F (37°C) and above, it unfolds a bit, losing that critical shape and thereby losing the ability to catalyze its step in the pathway to pigment. If the cells of the hair root are at that temperature or above, little or no pigment will be made and placed in the growing hair; if they are at a temperature below that, the mutant enzyme keeps its shape and functions in the production of pigment, producing pigmented hair. In the Siamese, only the skin of the "points"—face (mask), ears, feet, and tail—is cool enough for the mutant enzyme to work. The skin of the neck and body is normally too warm and very little pigment is made there. Because this mutation limits the amount of pigment formed, it is considered a case of partial albinism.

This is a good place to speak again of homozygosity and heterozygosity. If a cat is heterozygous for the gene under consideration, each of its cells will have a copy of the mutant allele and a copy of the wildtype allele. Since the wildtype allele will provide for wildtype enzyme, which is unimpaired by the normal range of body temperatures, there will be pigment in the hair all over the body. Because we can see the effect of the wildtype allele even when paired with the mutant allele, whose effect cannot be seen, we say that the wildtype is dominant to the mutant in this case. Only when a cat is homozygous for the mutant form, that is, when both alleles are the mutant form, will the effect of the mutation be evident, resulting in a cat with acromelanism, the Siamese or pointed coat.

Actually, studies of this coat pattern were first conducted and published using a breed of rabbit called Himalayan, which also shows pigment restriction to the points. Experimenters produced pigmented patches on Himalayan rabbits by strapping small ice packs to their backs for a time. Similarly, Siamese that stay outside in cold weather will turn dark all over. Conversely, if part of a point of a Himalayan rabbit or a Siamese cat is made warmer, the new hair there will be unpigmented. Experiments on Siamese cats were done by two Russian geneticists, N. A. and V. N. Iljin, who reported in 1930 in *The Journal of Heredity* the effects of both keeping Siamese in a cold environment and of bandaging a shaved area over the shoulders. The cold environment resulted in a darkening of the normally light-colored body. The bandage added warmth to the underlying shaved skin, which then produced unpigmented fur.

Color Variations

Natural changes in skin temperature will also upset the normal pattern. A very obese Siamese will have a darker body coat because the extra fat under the skin insulates the skin from the underlying body and its heat, making the skin cool enough to produce pigment. A head cold, with its inflammation of the membranes of the nose and sinuses, produces an elevated temperature in the skin of the face. The hair that is growing at that time will be unpig-mented, and, in a week or so, as it emerges, will give the mask a grizzled look.

Because the pigment-producing cells are also affected by certain hormones, there may be coloration changes brought about by changing length of days, which is detected by the nervous system, which in turn affects the endocrine system, and by pregnancy. Whatever the cause of these natural variations, the stunning contrast of dark and light coat will be regained after the tubby Siamese has slimmed down, the kittens are weaned, or the fever is a dim memory.

Coat Colors

In addition to the gene determining whether the color is all over (self) or restricted to the points (acromelanism), there are other genes that alter the molecular composition of the pigment and the way the pigment molecules are clumped into granules in the cells. These changes affect the way that the pigment in the hair shaft interacts with light and thus what color the hair appears to us. The interaction of these various genes produces the various point colors and patterns of the Siamese cat.

Basic Colors

There are four basic colors: seal point, chocolate point, blue point, and lilac point. These are recognized as Siamese by all of the cat registries and are eligible to be entered as such in their shows. Other point colors and patterns have been obtained by crossing Siamese with other breeds, such as American Shorthair, to get red color and tabby pattern. In some registries the resultant red points, cream points, tortie points, and all colors of lynx (tabbie) points are accepted as Siamese; in others they are considered a separate breed, Colorpoint Shorthair.

But seal point is the color that usually comes to mind when we say Siamese. It is considered the original or wildtype. Even so, there is variability in

that one color. The seal-point color may be a very dark brown to almost black, and the body an ivory to light sepia tint.

Gene Notation

Before we go on to the other colors, we need to learn some shorthand notation for the various genes and their alleles.

1. Color extent genes: The gene that governs the *ability to form color* is given the letter c, for color; its various alleles will all be labeled with variations of that letter. Since the wildtype, self, is dominant, it is given the capital letter C. The other alleles of this gene result in a reduction or complete lack of color and are called the albino series. The point restriction allele is c^s; the Burmese allele is c^b; c^a is given to the allele that in the homozygous condition produces white cats with pale blue eyes; and c is for the allele that in the homozygous condition produces the complete albino, the cat with white coat and red eyes. All of the albino series are recessive to the wildtype, which means that in order to show that type of coloring the cat must be homozygous for that allele. Thus we know that a Siamese or any cat that shows acromelanism must have two c^s alleles. In genetics shorthand this is written $c^s c^s$ and is called its genotype. One more genetics term: the physical expression of a genotype is called the phenotype. What you "see" (phenotype: pointed cat) comes from what you "got" (genotype: $c^s c^s$).

2. Black/brown gene: A different gene governs whether the basic color will be black or brown. The allele that produces black is dominant and designated by B. The other allele for this gene is b, which is recessive to B; when a cat is homozygous for this allele, bb, the color is brown. This is thought to be the result of a change in the construction of the pigment granules. In Siamese the black is called seal point and the brown is chocolate point. The point color of the chocolate ranges from dark brown (bittersweet) to light brown (milk chocolate); the body color is ivory.

Genetics

3. Density gene: Still another gene controls the distribution of the pigment granules in the cells. The wildtype allele, D, provides for the distribution of pigment granules throughout the cytoplasm of the cell and produces a full expression of whatever color is specified by the black/brown gene. It is dominant to the mutant allele, d, which in the homozygous state, dd, results in a clumping of the pigment granules around the nucleus in the center of the cell. With a microscope one can see the intense color around the nucleus and the surrounding colorless portion of the cell, but with the naked eye, the effect is to lighten or dilute the color of the hair. The dilution of black (seal point) produces slate gray (blue point), and the dilution of brown (chocolate point) produces lavender (lilac point). The body color of the blue point is a pale blue-gray, and of the lilac point, nearly white, with a pearly sheen.

Working with the genes described in 2. and 3., each of which has two alleles, four different point colors can be obtained:

Genotype	Phenotype
BBDD	seal point
BbDD	seal point
BBDd	seal point
BbDd	seal point

(These four genotypes can also be written as B_D_, with the _ standing for either allele of the gene, because the resulting phenotype will be the same whether the second allele for each gene is the wildtype or the mutant.)

bbD_	chocolate point
B_dd	blue point
bbdd	lilac point

The genes described in 1.–3. are all on regular (somatic) chromosomes. Most of the chromosomes of any animal are of this type, but mammals (and some other animals) also have a pair of sex chromosomes. The sex chromosomes are of two kinds: one is about the size of the average somatic chromosome and is called X; the other is much smaller and is called Y. An individual with two Xs (XX) is female and one with an X and a Y (XY) is male. In addition to genes that control the sex of the individual, there are other genes on these sex chromosomes that have nothing to do with sex. The Y, being so small, has just a few of these so-called sex-linked genes; the X has considerably more, and one of them contributes to the expression of color.

4. Orange gene: A gene on the X chromosome in its wildtype form allows the expression of whatever color is expected from the black/brown and density genes. Its mutant form converts the colors to orange, which is called red in most cat registries, or cream. We do not know what relationship the wildtype allele, o, has to the mutant, O, because all somatic cells have only one active X chromosome. This is obvious for the male, which has only one X per cell to start with, but females have two Xs. During the embryonic development of the female, one or the other of the X chromosomes is inactivated in each cell. This means that any gene on the X chromosome will have only one active allele in each cell, which is an exception to the rule of two of every kind of gene on the somatic chromosomes. In the ovary, however, the cells that will form the eggs or oocytes maintain two viable X chromosomes, each of which can be passed singly to an egg.

With the addition of the O allele the complexity of the possible phenotypes escalates. If you enjoy puzzles and word games, the fun starts here.

As a constant reminder that we are dealing with an X-linked gene, we will always write them as superscripts of X. Females can be X^oX^o, X^OX^o, or X^OX^O; males can be X^oY or X^OY. The most interesting of these genotypes is X^OX^o. In these females the coat will contain two colors: orange (red) or cream where the skin cells have inactivated X^o, and a color other than orange, depending on the other genes, where X^O has been inactivated.

41

This is called tortoiseshell in the self-patterned cat and tortie point in the Siamese.

Genotype	Phenotype
B_D_X°X°	seal-point female
B_D_X°Y	seal-point male
B_D_X°X°	red-point female
B_D_X°Y	red-point male
B_D_X°X°	seal tortie-point female
bbD_X°X°	chocolate-point female
bbD_X°Y	chocolate-point male
bbD_X°X°	cream-point female
bbD_X°Y	cream-point male
bbD_X°X°	chocolate-tortie point female
B_ddX°X°	blue-point female
B_ddX°Y	blue-point male
B_ddX°X°	cream-point female
B_ddX°Y	cream-point male
B_ddX°X°	blue-tortie point female
bbddX°X°	lilac-point female
bbddX°Y	lilac-point male
bbddX°X°	cream-point female
bbddX°Y	cream-point male
bbddX°X°	lilac-tortie point female

Additional Point-Color Patterns

From the above we see that with the introduction of the O allele another point-color pattern, tortie, was achieved, but only for females. Two other color patterns are possible with alleles of two other genes, agouti and tabby, brought in from other breeds.

Lynx and Patched Tabby Point

Cat geneticists and most breeders agree that all cats are tabbies. Those that do not show the stripes and whorls of contrasting color that we call tabby are the result of the action of a mutant allele of the agouti gene. The wildtype allele, A, of the agouti gene causes the hair to be banded with alternating zones of dark color and yellow. The overall result is a flecked, grayish color, such as the coat of the gray squirrel and the field mouse. The a allele of the agouti gene is recessive to the A; in the homozygous state it eliminates the yellow band so that the hair is solid colored. The aa genotype prevents the expression of the tabby gene. There are at least three alleles for the tabby gene; two of these affect the width of the yellow bands, while the third does not, leaving the agouti pattern more or less unchanged. The ones that change the width of the bands are T and T^b. The third one is T^a. T is the wildtype allele and produces the mackerel tabby, which has vertical stripes along the body. T^b is recessive to T; in the homozygous condition it produces the blotched (classic) tabby, which has a bull's-eye pattern on each side of the body. T^a, which is also recessive to T, in the homozygous state produces the ticked tabby, such as the Abyssinian cat, which usually has no stripes on the body and only a few darker markings elsewhere. The extremities of the mackerel and blotched tabbies have similar markings: lines around the eyes, an M on the forehead, bracelets on the legs, and rings on the tail. When T or T^b is introduced into the Siamese genotype, the points, but not the body, have the tabby markings, and the result is called lynx point. This pattern can be superimposed on any of the colors described above, producing seal lynx point to lilac lynx point. When the tabby pattern is combined with the tortie, the result is called tabby tortie point, patched tabby point, or tortie point.

Eye Color

Another startling feature of the Siamese is its blue eyes, also a result of the point restriction allele described above. The shade of blue ranges from a pale china-blue to a deep blue-violet. The color is a result of a reduced amount of pigment in the iris, caused by the partial albinism of the $c^s c^s$ genotype, the scattering of light by the colloidal substance within the eye, and the reflection of light from the retina. The seal points tend to have the deepest shades of blue and the lilac point the lightest.

Making Crosses

Punnett Squares

Knowing about genetics is fun, but using genetics is greater fun. Using the information above, we can predict what colors are possible and how likely they are to turn up in a litter. The device for this is called the Punnett square. For example, suppose we want to see what colors are possible from a lilac-point male and a seal-point female that had had a lilac-point parent. By just looking at the seal point we know that it is B_D_; by looking at its pedigree we know further that it is BdDd because of its lilac-point parent, bbdd. When gametes develop, the cells divide in such a way that the final products, the egg cells and the sperm cells, have a single set of chromosomes, and thus one copy of each and every gene. To set up the Punnett square we first write the genotypes of the parents: BbDd X bbdd.

Next, we draw two lines that cross.

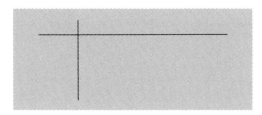

The possible classes of eggs (with respect to the two genes in question) will be aligned vertically to the left, and the possible classes of sperm will be arranged horizontally above the line. For the female there are four possible classes of eggs: BD, Bd, bD, and bd. (Remember that each gamete gets one and only one of each kind of gene.) Since the male is homozygous for both genes, he has only one class of sperm: bd. Now, we write in the gamete classes and draw lines between them, making a grid.

	bd
BD	
Bd	
bD	
bd	

We bring together the classes of eggs and sperm in the empty boxes, combine their letters, and get the possible offspring genotypes.

	bd
BD	BdDd
Bd	Bbdd
bD	bbDd
bd	bbdd

From this we see that the possibilities are seal point, chocolate point, blue point, and lilac point; furthermore, the fact that there is one box for each genotype tells us that the chances of any one of these is one in four.

From the genotypes above and these examples you can make any cross and predict the colors and expected ratios of the kittens, but if puzzles and genotypes are not your idea of fun, a quick-and-easy genetics table follows.

Genetics

Genetics Table for Coat Colors

Use the numbers of the phenotypes listed below to find the possible phenotypes of offspring in the table. For example, a lilac-point sire (4) and a red-point dam (5) could have female (F) kittens of phenotypes 7, 8, 9, and 10 and male (M) kittens of 5 and 6.

1. seal point	6. cream point
2. blue point	7. tortie point
3. chocolate point	8. blue-cream (blue tortie) point
4. lilac point	9. chocolate-tortie point
5. red point	10. lilac-tortie point

Sire / Dam	1	2	3	4	5	6
1	1–4	1–4	1–4	1–4	F 7–10 M 1–4	F 7–10 M 1–4
2	1–4	2, 4	1–4	2, 4	F 7–10 M 1–4	F 7–10 M 1–4
3	1–4	1–4	3, 4	3, 4	F 7–10 M 1–4	F 7–10 M 1–4
4	1–4	2, 4	3, 4	4	F 7–10 M 1–4	F 8, 10 M 2, 4
5	F 7–10 M 5, 6	F 7–10 M 5, 6	F 7–10 M 5, 6	F 7–10 M 5, 6	5, 6	5, 6
6	F 7–10 M 5, 6	F 8, 10 M 6	F 7–10 M 5, 6	F 8, 10 M 6	5, 6	5, 6
7	F 1–4, 7–10 M 1–6	F 1–4, 7–10 M 1–6	F 1–4, 7–10 M 1–6	F 1–4, 7–10 M 1–6	F 5–10 M 1–6	F 5–10 M 1–6
8	F 1–4, 7–10 M 1–6	F 2, 4, 8, 10 M 2, 4, 6	F 1–4, 7–10 M 1–6	F 2, 4, 8, 10 M 2, 4, 6	F 5–10 M 1–6	F 6, 8, 10 M 1–6
9	F 1–4, 7–10 M 1–6	F 1–4, 7–10 M 1–6	F 3, 4, 9, 10 M 3–6	F 3, 4, 9, 10 M 3–6	F 5–10 M 1–6	F 5–10 M 1–6
10	F 1–4, 7–10 M 1– 6	F 2, 4, 8, 10 M 2, 4, 6	F 3, 4, 9, 10 M 3–6	F 4, 10 M 4, 6	F 5–10 M 1–6	F 6, 8, 10 M 2, 4, 6

Above left: Red points almost always show tabby barring. ▶ This one has a long head and lovely profile.
Above right: The large, slightly too round eyes of this blue cream point give it an especially appealing look.
Below: Seal tortie points are almost always females. This one shows the pattern as shading on the body.

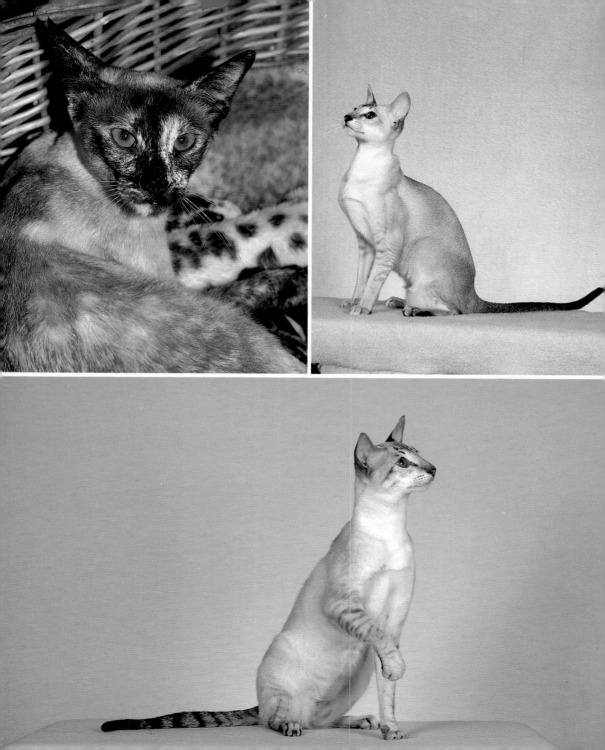

Breeding

Now comes the hard part. Crosses on paper are easy and entertaining, but real-life breeding does not always produce expected results with happy endings. This section may be a bit strong to take, but it should help you decide whether you really want to get into breeding.

Basic Concerns

Often the novice breeder expects no difficulties in breeding a pedigreed cat. This may be because of the erroneous idea that cats in general, based on what we see of outdoor cats, have an easy time of it. The nonpedigreed cat may have fewer difficulties in kittening, but not as few as are evident to the casual observer. After all, when the outdoor female has difficulty in giving birth, she dies. We don't know about it. When her newborn kittens need help in getting started, they die, and we don't know about it.

Another source of concern for the pedigreed female is the generations of artificial selection. In the paragraph above we see natural selection, however harsh, at work. In the pedigreed cats, we have substituted a measure of artificial selection, not only in how they look, but in our assistance in the delivery and rearing of kittens. So we must be prepared to continue to assist if we want to assure the safety of the mother and kits.

Preparations Before Mating

Once you have decided to breed your Siamese female, there are many details to take care of in advance. First, she should be in good health and up to date with all her immunizations. A suitable

◄ Above left: A seal tortie point, Black Iron's Tuppence, bred and owned by Kathleen Abbot.
Above right: Seal lynx points have bracelets, tail stripes, and facial lines of seal color.
Below: The slight receding chin, smaller ears, and shorter tail of this seal lynx point are the result of the non-Siamese component in its heritage.

male must be located and arrangements made for his service. Thought should be given to the disposition of the kittens. Timing of the breeding is very important.

The Health of the Queen

The health of the female, called a queen or catta, is your first concern. She should be free of parasites, well nourished, and healthy. A visit to your veterinarian for a checkup is a good idea. At the same time, have all her immunizations boosted, as some cannot be given to pregnant cats and you want her immunity as strong as possible for herself and the kittens. If you do not own your own stud, you will probably need a recent feline leukemia test or certificate of vaccination against leukemia. The owner of the male, the stud cat, may require evidence of other tests also.

Finding a Suitable Stud

If you do not have your own stud, finding one can be as involved as getting a cat or kitten in the first place. Many beginning breeders go back to the breeder of their female for stud service. This offers certain advantages: You already know the person and you know something about that person's cattery. If this is not possible, then you will need to search for a male through breeders' advertisements in cat magazines and newspapers and at cat shows. The yearbooks of the various cat registries are another good source of information.

Before you begin searching for a male, you should have some idea about the qualities that you want. Do you require that the male be purebred? Must he be registered? Must he be free of faults that could be passed on to his offspring and prevent them from being shown? Do you require that he be a champion or grand champion? What colors would be acceptable? What particular characteristics of form and personality do you want? Should he be a proven male? What health guarantees do you want? And, finally, what is the maximum stud fee you are willing to pay?

Breeding

The answers to the first three or four questions will depend on your purpose in breeding. If you plan to breed your female only once and have homes waiting for up to seven kittens that cannot be registered or shown and that may turn out to have white toes, then you may not be interested in whether the stud cat is registered or not. On the other hand, if you plan to establish yourself as a breeder of registerable, showable Siamese kittens, these are essential considerations. Let us address them.

The stud should be registered. If he is not, his offspring cannot be registered, no matter the qualifications of the queen. The owner of the male should be able to show you the stud's registration certificate. This certificate carries his name, the names of his sire and dam, his birth date, his point color, his registration number, the name of the owner, the signature or seal of the appropriate official of that registry, and the name of the registry—all on a white slip of paper that is usually about 8½ x 4 inches. This information is minimal. It assures you that, barring some erroneous registration in the past, the cat in question has only Siamese in its pedigree. It should rule out the possibility of coming up with kittens that have unSiamese faults, such as white toes. It does not rule out the possibility of Siamese-type faults, such as crossed eyes and kinked tails. A certificate of championship helps. This tells you that at the time he was shown he had no set, serious faults and achieved at least 90 of the 100 points in the Siamese breed standard as determined on four or more occasions by the judges who awarded the championship wins. A certificate of grand championship or higher provides even greater assurance of lack of faults and higher conformance to the breed standard. (This will be more evident in the chapter on showing.)

However desirable, certificates cannot substitute for seeing the prospective bridegroom himself. It is not unusual to ask for photographs of him, especially if he is at some distance from you. If the pictures are pleasing, then, if at all possible, you should arrange to visit him and his owner. This will allow you to see where he lives and where your queen will be kept, as the queens almost always travel to the stud, and will provide an opportunity for you and the stud's owner to come to terms.

The Genetic Traits of the Stud

Before you decide on a particular stud, try to decide what traits are needed to complement your queen's traits. If she has an exceptionally long, whippy tail then, while it would be desirable in the stud, it would not be at the top of the list. If, however, her ears are a bit too small, then his need to be large, and so on. Do not forget personality. While much of a Siamese's lovingness depends on its early life with humans, there is a genetic component to the ability to trust people. Studies by geneticists on both dogs and cats support this, as do my own observations. Many years ago we got a beautiful Siamese kitten from friends, who we knew did all the right things with their cats and kittens. This lovely girl brought many desirable traits to our cattery and through her our Siamese became more beautiful, but she was a very fearful cat. Only when she was pregnant or nursing kittens did she trust us, and then she was very loving towards us. At other times, she ran from us on sight, despite all our years together. Her breeders told us that this behavior could be traced back to one of the cat's grandmothers, whom we shall call Merry Widow. We bred our fearful cat to a male who was the opposite in personality and kept one of their daughters, who also inherited what we called the Merry Widow gene, but was much less fearful than her mother. Finally, with the next generation, again breeding to a very trusting male, the fearfulness was eliminated.

Experience and Fertility

Now we come to the last three questions posed above. Should he be a proven stud, that is, have already sired at least one litter? It is highly recommended, especially if this is your queen's first breeding. Putting two inexperienced Siamese together can be frustrating for all concerned. More importantly, the proven stud is less likely to be sterile.

Other than fertility, what health guarantees should you require? It is usual to ask for a certificate that the cat has had a negative feline leukemia test within the last three months or an earlier test followed by vaccination against leukemia. In addition, some are now asking for proof of a negative feline immunosuppressive virus (FIV) test and vaccination against feline infectious peritonitis (FIP). Again, certificates are assurances of good health, but should be supplemented with your own keen eyes. Look him over as carefully as you looked at kittens when you got your female. The eyes and the coat are the most obvious indicators of health. (Review that portion of Chapter One for details.) Ask the owner to handle the stud as you observe them so that you can see how the cat responds. This will also allow you to better judge the stud's condition. Look for a tight, smooth abdomen and sides and easy, powerful movement.

The Stud Fee

And finally, the matter of the stud fee. The amount is set by the owner of the stud and will depend on what value she or he sets on the service. For a registered male without championship, the fee is usually a few hundred dollars; for a top show male, it could be in the thousands. Do not expect to offer a kitten in lieu of a fee; this sort of exchange is rare and when it does occur, it is usually between established breeders who have known each other for years. For the fee, your queen is also entitled to a return service if she does not conceive the first time. At one time, stud owners would guarantee a live birth, that is, even if the queen conceived but the pregnancy failed to produce a single live kitten, the queen might return for another breeding without charge, but this is disappearing from the scene. The owner of the stud may have a standard contract, or the two of you may write out a simple statement of the terms, which should include the agreement of the stud's owner to sign the litter registration forms.

Usually the fee is paid when you go to pick up the queen after the breeding; if they do not mate there should be no fee.

Timing

Timing, as in everything, is critical. First, the age of the queen: She should be at least one year old before being bred for the first time to be sure that she is fully grown. Siamese females usually come into heat (estrus) before then, but it's a good idea to wait for that first birthday. The waiting time can be spent in the preparations outlined above.

The time of year is important if the kittens are going to be sold. Kittens that are ready to go to new homes in the summer are at a disadvantage—too many vacation trips are being planned. A better time to sell kittens is from September through December. This means breedings from January through April are best avoided.

The best laid plans come to nought, however, if the female does not go into heat. Her cycles are seasonal and, all other factors being normal, are triggered by twelve or more hours of daylight per day. Hormone therapy can bring on estrus, but such treatment is rarely needed with Siamese.

The timing of the breeding during the heat cycle is very important. Cats do not ovulate spontaneously, as many species do; instead, ovulation is induced by copulation. Each mating does not always result in ovulation. Recent evidence indicates that the most critical time in the heat cycle is the third through fourth day. Several matings on these days are needed to trigger the hormonal changes that bring about ovulation and to prepare the uterine lining for implantation.

If you are going out for stud service it is essential that arrangements be made in advance. The stud's owner will want to have a general idea of when your female will be coming to the stud and, when that fateful heat begins, should be called immediately. The second day of heat is the best one for transporting the female to the stud; earlier than that the stress of travel can interrupt the estrus before it gets well underway, and later, it can terminate that cycle prematurely. Even with travel on the second day, the female will be thrown out of heat for a while. She should be caged near the stud, so that they can see and smell each other. Usually by the next morning they are both ready for the honeymoon. Even when both seem ready, the first meeting should be chaperoned. I have seen females attack the stud, and more rarely, vice versa. Once a feisty little female in heat attacked me. Since then I keep a clean dustmop handy for separating fighters and defending myself. A throw rug can be useful, too. (Olé!)

Mating

Most breeders allow the pair to be together on four or five days, separating them at night to give everyone a rest and the opportunity to eat. During their time together several matings should be observed to completion as there is no other way to be certain that their efforts have been successful. Carpeting or a large throw rug should be provided for the breeding area. The male usually sits up very tall and sings to the female first. She may roll on the floor or crouch. When he sees his opportunity he will lunge for the back of her neck and take a mouthful of the loose (and tough) skin there. Her response is to crouch low and move her tail to one side. The male then steps on one of her thighs repeatedly, which causes the female to elevate her hindquarters and allows completion of the mating. As the act is completed the female lets out a roar, but such a sound alone is not enough to be sure of the mating, as I have occasionally witnessed an incomplete coupling that ended with a roar from the female.

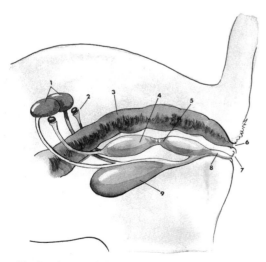

The female urogenital system.

1. kidney
2. ovaries
3. large intestine
4. uterus
5. cervix
6. anus
7. vulva
8. vagina
9. bladder

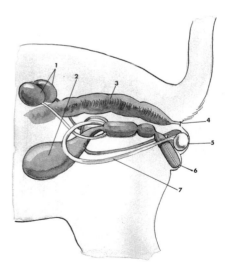

The male urogenital system.

1. kidney
2. bladder
3. large intestine
4. anus
5. testicles
6. penis
7. vas deferens

Breeding

Post-Mating Concerns

After the female is separated from the male, she may continue in heat for several more days, but with lessening intensity, as breeding does not shorten the heat period. The skin of her neck should be examined carefully for infection from the bites of the male. These bites do not usually break the skin, but sometimes they do. Even when no surface damage is apparent, feel for swellings under the skin, as nasty abscesses can develop from very small punctures. At any sign of infection take her to the veterinarian at once.

Now the waiting begins. Not all matings result in pregnancy. There are many possible reasons for failure, including failure to ovulate and sterility of the stud. If the mating was unsuccessful, the female will go back into heat in one to three weeks, unless she has a pseudopregnancy, which is a rarity in cats and will last 30 to 45 days, after which she will go into heat after one or two weeks. In either case, the owner of the stud should be contacted if you wish to have a return service for your queen.

Signs of Pregnancy

Usually the first signs of pregnancy are a pinking and enlargement of the nipples at three to four weeks, but sometimes the queen will have morning sickness, vomiting a small amount of clear stomach fluid before breakfast, within a week or so. At 16 to 30 days the embryos in their membranes are like little balls at intervals in the uterus. At this time they can be palpated (felt), but this should be done *only* by a veterinarian and *only* for a good reason. Before this time, the fetuses are too small to be felt, and later they elongate and fill the uterine horns like stuffed sausages and are difficult to distinguish from one another until after 45 or so days. The caution about any palpation is not because of the difficulty of feeling the kittens, but because of the real danger of damaging the uterus or kittens. Palpation can cause abortion. Ultrasound can be used to diagnose pregnancy after 17 days and X-rays, after 38 to 40 days.

Gestation

The average gestation time for Siamese is about 65 days, counting from the first day of mating, which is about a week longer than for the nonpedigreed, domestic cat. The time may vary quite a bit from queen to queen, even among close relatives, but a queen will usually carry for the same time, plus or minus a day, for each of her litters. My first Siamese litter was a nail-biter. One of the cat-care books said that if the female went beyond 69 days there was something seriously wrong. Poopsie hit 70 days and no sign of labor. We rushed her over to the Animal Medical Center, where an examination including X-ray showed nothing wrong and five kittens waiting to be born. We were told to go home and wait. The next morning at 8:00, Poopsie woke me up and proceeded to deliver five normal, healthy kittens at fifteen-minute intervals, finishing at 9:00 a.m. on her 71st day. I threw that book away.

Predicting the Birthdate

Despite the natural variability in gestation times, it is very important to know the date of the first mating. Using that date as time zero, an approximate birthdate can be calculated. For example, if the first mating was on December 2, 65 days later would be February 5—29 days of December, 31 of January, and 5 of February. Not only is this necessary to prepare for a normal delivery, but should anything go wrong at any time during the pregnancy, the veterinarian will need to know exactly how far along she is.

Nutrition

Those 65 or so days can seem like an eternity, especially to the first-time breeder. There are a number of things to do that not only help pass the time, but contribute to a healthy gestation and safe delivery. Foremost of these is providing proper nutrition for the queen and the developing kittens. Fortunately, that is not difficult these days, and there are many commercial cat foods that are suitable. Basically, the sound diet (which is discussed in the chapter on nutrition) that she was on before the breeding should be continued. Studies have shown that increasing the caloric content of the diet immediately after breeding can lead to death of the embryos. Her appetite may not increase for the first few weeks, but as it does, more food should be made available to her. In fact, during the last half of the pregnancy, I find that having dry food available at all times works well for my queens. Not one has ever become obese during pregnancy, and it relieves my anxiety about being late with their evening meal. Feline researchers recommend that after the pregnancy is diagnosed, which may be at three to four weeks at the earliest, her calorie intake be increased by one-third and her diet be at least 30% protein.

To supplement or not to supplement the complete diet is controversial. Twenty years ago it was considered the correct thing to do; mineral and vitamin supplements were given routinely to the healthy, pregnant cat. This practice diminished, however, as breeders found that too much of a good thing can be detrimental—kittens were growing too large before birth. At the same time, cat-food manufacturers were improving the mineral and vitamin content of their products. Read the cat-food labels carefully and consult your veterinarian. It is very important that her diet contain adequate vitamin A; a deficiency can result in failure of implantation and embryonic death in early stages and cleft palate in older stages. I no longer use dietary supplements, except as occasional treats or when something interferes with the normal intake of food. If, for example, toward the end of her pregnancy, the female seems unable to eat a normal amount at each meal because of the crowded situation inside, offer her one of the high-calorie, low-volume supplements in a tube, such as Nutri-Cal.

Disease

Obviously, the queen should not be exposed to sick cats or people. Should she pick up a head cold or show other signs of illness, take her to the veterinarian at once. Be sure to tell him, of course, that she is pregnant and how far advanced. Certain antibiotics are safe to use during pregnancy, but in general, avoid all medications, including worm treatments, vaccinations, and insecticides.

Stress

Also important to the good health of the queen is the avoidance of unnecessary stress. Keep her happy. For any cat this means physical freedom in her domain and a life of routine—having everything the same way and the way she wants it every day, including the proper ration of human attention. And no big surprises, please. This would not be the time to add a large, boisterous puppy to the pet family.

Exercise

This is not to say the queen should be treated as an invalid. I have heard of breeders who confine their females to cages as soon as they are bred for fear of loss of the kittens from the queen jumping or running; this is terribly misguided. She should be allowed to follow her instincts as to activity and rest; if she wants to run up and down stairs or climb to the top of the cat tree, let her. When she gets to the later stages, she will slow down on her own.

Final Weeks of Pregnancy

A noticeable change in the queen's girth may not occur until rather late in the pregnancy—six weeks or so, depending to some extent on the number of kittens. While the developing kittens, called fetuses from 28 days to birth, have all their organs at four weeks, they are only 1 inch or 2.5 cm long. At five to six weeks they are about 2½ inches or 6 cm long. Despite the temptation to try to determine how many kittens are on the way, do not try to palpate them. Remember, palpation can cause abortion if attempted at the wrong time or if done too forcefully.

Activity of the Kittens

The fastest growth of the fetuses will take place during the last two weeks, reaching a birth length of about 4 inches or 10 cm from the crown of the head to the rump, which is a bit smaller than the average, nonpedigreed kitten. During this time, the queen's body will assume a distinctly bumpy look, and the movements of the kittens should become evident. Just by resting a hand lightly on her side you should be able to feel their calisthenics. Another way is to hold the queen on your lap. And it is not uncommon to see their movements from several feet away. Should the queen need veterinary care, it is helpful to know when kitten activity was last noted. But kittens, like human babies, have inactive (sleep) periods, too, so do not expect movement all the time.

Changes in the Queen

While you are monitoring kitten activity, continue to be alert to the queen's condition also. It is normal to see increases in her food and water intake and increases in urine output and defecation throughout the pregnancy. During the last week, it is normal for her to have occasional uterine contractions; these cause her sides to become quite hard, but are not a cause for alarm as long as they are only occasional and not accompanied by a discharge. It is not normal for her to refuse to eat, except perhaps just before labor begins. Any discharge from the vagina, other than the normal "show" of blood at the beginning of labor, is a danger signal. Elevated third eyelids (haws), spikey fur, vomiting, diarrhea, prolonged and intense premature uterine contractions, and any other sign of illness or abnormal behavior should be reported immediately to the veterinarian.

The Nesting Box

Two or three weeks before the due date she will probably welcome a nesting box. I recommend a clean cardboard box that has not held anything noxious. The box should be of such a size that the queen can lie comfortably on her side with outstretched legs and stand up without bumping her head on the top. Look for one whose top has been opened by cutting on three sides, making a solid flap top. On the side opposite to the one that was not detached from the top cut out a semicircle just large enough for her to enter the box. Put in some temporary bedding such as paper toweling and a few clean rags. Place the box in a quiet place and bring the queen over. She should be drawn like a magnet to the small, dark, secret chamber. If not, it could be that she wants it in a more private spot or that the nesting instinct has not been turned on yet. Once the nesting box is accepted, she will spend time in it every day, first tearing up the bedding (we call this redecorating the nursery) and then lying contentedly on the mess.

Assistance with Grooming

This brings us to the last week. By now, the queen may be so large that she cannot groom herself after using the litter box and will need help keeping herself clean. Accumulation of urine on the vulva is usually more of a problem than fecal material around the anus, as the normal movements are firm enough to leave no soil. In either case, dampen a pad of toilet tissue or a cotton ball with warm water and gently wipe the soiled area, then dry it with tissue.

Preparations for the Delivery

By this time you should have assembled the following supplies for assisting at the delivery (queening):

1. Betadine solution
2. rubbing alcohol (70% methanol)
3. small scissors, preferably blunt-tipped
4. fresh, unopened roll of plain white paper towels
5. fresh, unopened box of unscented white tissues
6. dieter's food scales, calibrated in ounces

7. precut 6-inch lengths of thread of different colors
8. fresh, unopened tube or jar of petroleum jelly
9. thin, surgical-type rubber gloves
10. freshly laundered bedding of old sheets or receiving blankets (not terrycloth)
11. food coloring
12. cotton-tipped swabs
13. pad of writing paper and pencil
14. clock
15. veterinarian's telephone numbers
16. synthetic cat's milk
17. medicine dropper and/or Catac nurser with smallest nipples

Labor and Delivery

Signs of Labor

Well, we are now ready for the kitten-stork, but how to know when he will arrive? The only sure way is to take the queen's temperature every morning; on the day she will deliver, her temperature will be a degree or so below the normal 102°F (40°C). Other signs include refusing to eat, wanting her person to stay with her at the nesting box, sudden loud cries, and a bloody discharge. The surest sign, of course, is the onset of uterine contractions. In true labor these will increase in strength and frequency. In false labor they will not become strong, "bearing down" contractions and will cease after a few minutes. Do not leave the measure of contractions to subjective observations; use items 13 and 14 above to note and record times and intensity of contractions.

If at all possible, have an assistant, particularly if you and the queen are doing all this for the first time. My husband has been pressed into service many times as note taker, handholder, conferrer, coffee provider, and, occasionally, as ambulance driver. (When labor starts he always says he's catching the next flight to Miami.)

Early Labor

Once the queen goes into labor, arrange flat layers of newspaper and cloths in the nest box. It is a good idea to leave at least some of the original cloths in it, because they have her odor on them. When she has settled into the box, I cover my bed with an old sheet and put the nest box with queen inside in the middle of the bed, as sitting on the floor for hours is not easy for humans. The remainder of the supplies should be put out on the bed or a nearby table. Submerge the scissor's blades and the lengths of thread in rubbing alcohol. Open the paper towels and tissues. Scrub your hands hard, particularly around and under the nails, using a brush and soap. After rinsing well with running water, rinse your hands with some of the alcohol and dry them with the paper toweling. After the scissors and thread have been in the alcohol at least five minutes, place them on a pad of paper towels on the bedside table and let them air-dry.

Hard Labor

Unfortunately, there is no simple rule to follow about when to seek help for a laboring queen. Years ago the rule was that after one hour of labor and no kitten, get her to the veterinarian. That needs to be redefined. The early stages of labor can go on for several hours. What has to be watched carefully is the time she is in hard labor, that is, when the contractions are very heavy and come in twos and threes. The queen's whole body heaves with them; sometimes her vibrissae (whiskers) arch together in front of her face with the contraction. If no kitten is forthcoming after an hour of such contractions at two- to three-minute intervals, it's ambulance time. If the queen appears exhausted between contractions even before an hour has passed or if bright red blood is being passed steadily, it's time to seek help. Some blood mixed with uterine fluids is normal, but this should not be as bright or dark as undiluted blood. Checking the color of the discharge is best done with white tissues or paper towels, as this allows you to best judge whether it is a blood and fluid mixture or all blood.

Dystocia

If the queen has difficulty, remember the word dystocia (diss-TOE-see-ah). It means difficult birth and will get your cat help faster than any other single word. I still see us hurrying up the indoor ramp at the Animal Medical Center years ago and hear the downstairs receptionist calling up, "Dystocia on the way!" and our suffering queen being taken directly into an examining room without paper work, past all the other patients.

Should a Caesarean section be required, expect to lose at least some of the kittens; they just do not survive the anesthesia. (Be sure to request inhalation anesthesia; even adult Siamese are extremely sensitive to Ketamine and other injectables.) It is not necessary to have the queen spayed at the same time, nor is it certain that future deliveries will require surgery.

Normal Delivery

But let us hope that dystocia remains just a curious word and not a reality, in which case, the first kitten slips out with no difficulty. If all goes well, after an hour or less of strong labor, a bubble

A queen giving birth. Note the just-delivered kitten in its membranous sac.

of fluid-filled membrane will appear or, if the membrane surrounding the kitten is burst during labor, a gush of clear fluid. Next, some part of the kitten will show. If it's the head, the kitten is usually delivered with two or three sets of contractions, but half the time it's breech, with the hindquarters coming first. This usually takes longer and can be nerve-wracking. I remember once that a kitten presented with a back foot out and took so long that the foot, which must have had its circulation impeded, swelled up three times normal size and turned blue. Fortunately, after the kitten was delivered, the foot returned to normal.

Minor Assistance

There are times when the kitten is partly out but the next set of contractions does not expel it further. Items 8 and 9 can help; put on the rubber gloves and apply some of the petroleum jelly between the kitten and the wall of the vagina. A friend once used cooking oil in such an emergency, and the kitten shot out at the next contraction. If enough of the kitten is exposed, you can wrap a tissue or paper towel around it and pull very gently with the next contraction. Often, when the presentation is breech the kitten is delivered all but the head. Sometimes the kitten starts struggling while its head is still in the birth canal; a gentle pull with the next contraction will complete the delivery.

Once the kitten is out, the queen will usually lick the membrane away and begin washing the kitten's face. The next set of contractions delivers the placenta; when she detects it, she may eat it and then go on to sever the umbilical cord. (Keep an eye on this process as some do not know when to stop.) Do not stop her if she wants to eat the placenta; it is a rich source of nutrients and hormones that are beneficial to her at this point. If she does not immediately free the kitten from its sac and fluids, you must do it. Simply pinch a portion of the sac and rip it open. Quickly wipe away the fluid from the kitten's nose and mouth with a tissue. By this time the kitten should be moving and breathing, and its placenta

Breeding

Giving birth. Washing the newborn removes the sac and fluids, dries its coat, and stimulates respiration.

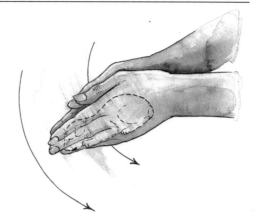

Slinging a newborn kitten to rid the respiratory passages of fluid.

should have been delivered. If it is breathing without difficulty, but the placenta is not out, just wait. Do not pull on the kitten; it could cause an umbilical hernia. If it is having difficulty breathing or if the placenta is not delivered in about five minutes, carefully cut the umbilical cord as close to the vulva as possible while pinching tightly on the kitten side of the cord. When you release the cord there may be a drop or two of blood lost without danger to the kitten. If the placenta is passed before you cut the cord, milk the cord toward the kitten before cutting it so that it gets as much blood as possible returned to its body. There is smooth muscle in the cord that normally performs this function by contracting and constricting the cord. If it continues to bleed, tie it off about one-half inch from the kitten with a piece of thread. If the kitten's breathing sounds gurgly, hold it immobilized between your hands with its head between your fingertips and its body between your palms and gently sling downward to get rid of the fluid in its airways. Wipe its nose and mouth again. Present it to the queen for further cleaning.

Resuscitation

Should the newborn appear lifeless, do not give up on it. Clear its airways by slinging its head down as you hold it between your hands and then rub its sides and back. Blow very gently into its mouth or alternately raise and lower its arms to ventilate the lungs. If you cannot detect a heartbeat, lightly thump the chest. I'll never forget a kitten called Lazarus, who was born to a first-time queen while I was at work. When I got home, two kittens had been delivered; one was nursing and the other was lying, cold and limp, with absolutely no sign of life, at the side of the nest box. Its membranes had been removed, but it was wet and the placenta was still attached. I picked it up to check for birth defects; on the topside everything looked all right. When I turned it over to check its palate, it gaped. Well, I shifted to high gear. I warmed and stimulated it with a wet washcloth, scrubbing it backwards and forwards, raising and lowering its arms repeatedly to ventilate its lungs. By this time the mother was delivering the third kitten, and I was home alone. To make a harrowing story short, after an hour the kitten was functioning on its own, and in two hours was nursing. It turned out to be a perfectly normal cat and is living happily ever after in Connecticut.

Breeding

Placentas

Be sure to keep track of the number of placentas that are expelled. A retained placenta can lead to serious infection and death of the queen. Normally, there is one placenta per kitten, but occasionally there are twins that share a placenta. This can be determined by following the umbilical cords to their junction with the placenta. Do *not* try to pull the placenta out; it must turn loose from the uterine wall on its own. Pulling on it could tear the uterus and result in the immediate death of the queen.

Postnatal Care

Once the kitten is out and breathing well, douse the umbilical cord with Betadine solution, especially at the cut end. Until the cord dries it is a pathway for bacteria into the abdominal cavity of the kitten, which can lead to peritonitis and death of the kitten. The Betadine tends to roll off the cord, so I really pour it on and repeat the application several times.

Weight

Now is the time to weigh the kitten. The average Siamese kitten is around 3 ounces (90 gms) at birth, which is smaller than nonpedigreed kittens. It is very important to record the weight of each kitten and to be able to tell the kittens apart. Remember, their coloring is temperature-sensitive, so at birth they are all white because their hair developed at the interior temperature of the queen. That's where the food coloring and cotton swabs come in. Mark each kitten under an arm with the coloring and record its birth data on the note pad. (Underarms are the site of choice as they get washed least frequently by the queen.) A typical birth entry would look like this:

Time	Sex	Weight	Code	Placenta Delivered
0840	M	3.25 oz	red, right	yes

Sexing kittens. The male, on left; the female, on the right.

Although most scales do not read out to quarters of an ounce, I estimate the fractions. Determining the sex may have to wait until later. If the anus and genital opening look like a colon (:), it's a male; if they look more like a semicolon (;), it's a female.

The Nest

As the kittens are born, much amniotic fluid and some blood will soak the bedding. To keep the nest fairly dry without disturbing the queen, I start out with several paper towels under her hindquarters. As these get wet, I replace them with dry ones.

While the newborn kittens should be kept warm, do *not* use a heating pad or hot-water bottles under them or the queen. Even wrapped in cloths these can cause burns to the queen and death of the kittens. As long as the kitten box is in a warm, draft-free room, additional heating is not necessary. If you feel some heat must be added, position a lamp nearby.

The Queen

When all the kittens are delivered, the queen usually washes herself and lies back, tired, but obviously happy. If she ate the placentas, she will not be hungry for some time, but you should offer her water and then place the dish nearby. She may still appear larger than normal. Sometimes this is the result of intestinal gas or just the bulk of the uterus, but sometimes it's because there are more to come. Raisinette delivered two kittens on Saturday morning, after which labor stopped. She behaved absolutely normally—feeding the kittens, eating, using her litter box. But Monday morning there were two more kittens in the nest!

Congenital Defects

As each kitten is born I check it for congenital defects. Fortunately, these are rare in litters born to healthy Siamese. Not all of them are serious, nor are all genetic. Illness, poor nutrition, and exposure to certain medications and other chemicals during the pregnancy can cause abnormalities, but often the cause is unknown—just an accident in development. If the newborn has a serious defect, such as an organ outside the body, it should be taken to the veterinarian for euthanasia. Some of these might be saved by surgery, but it would be costly and the outcome very uncertain.

Cleft Palate

A defect that can be accommodated until a time that surgery can be performed is cleft palate. In some species cleft palate appears to be a genetic defect; in cats it can be caused by insufficient vitamin A during development. The kitten with the cleft palate may not be able to nurse the queen or may have great difficulty nursing, depending on the severity, since the oral cavity and nasal cavity are confluent. It can be hand-fed by gastric tube or with the use of a special nipple until such time as surgical repair is possible. Again, the owner, with the veterinarian's advice, must weigh the costs and outcomes.

Minor Defects

Umbilical hernias and club feet are not serious birth defects. The hernia, which shows as a bulge at the navel, is not life-threatening and is very simple to repair later. What looks like club feet are not truly club feet in kittens, but a distortion of the hind foot resulting from the leg being caught for some time in an abnormal position in the uterus. The first (and only) time I saw this my heart sank. The back foot was doubled inward across the long part of the foot, halfway between the hock and the toes. My first thought was euthanasia, but she was otherwise healthy and nursed vigorously. I started calling other breeders. One said, "Oh, yes! One of mine had that. Just splint it with the end of a popsicle stick, and it will be fine." Well, I couldn't keep the stick on her foot, but I kept straightening it by hand many times a day, which was not difficult and seemed to cause her no pain. And sure enough, Foot's foot straightened out, leaving no vestige of deformity. Her cousin Cleo and she, now known as Samantha, are living happily in Brooklyn.

Nursing

Getting the kittens to start nursing is the next concern. Again, there is great variability among newborns. I remember one kitten who was searching for a nipple before his umbilical cord was cut; others seem sleepy and uninterested, and still others search unsuccessfully, passing over nipple after nipple without latching on. Kittens are attracted to the nipples by smell, so it is not a good idea to wash them. Sometimes squeezing a drop of milk out and then putting the kitten's mouth to it seems to help. Usually within two to three hours all are nursing. For the first week or so they tend to stay with one nipple; later they nurse on any of them.

Colostrum

During the last week of pregnancy the breast tissue swells up and a whitish fluid may be expressible on the last day. This is colostrum, not true milk. It is higher in protein, vitamin A, and minerals and lower in fat than milk. It also contains antibodies, which are probably digested in the kitten's intestine, but which may help protect against bacterial infection in the digestive tract. In a day or two, the queen begins producing true milk.

Difficulties

Two things can go wrong at this point: The queen may have no colostrum or milk or she may refuse to have anything to do with the kittens. If she is dry, call the veterinarian. A hormone injection can usually get milk production started. If she refuses the kittens, try getting her odor onto them by putting some of her urine or vaginal secretions on their backs, or transfer her cheek scent to them by stroking the sides of her face and then the kittens. Another trick is to present the rear end of the kitten, particularly after stimulating it to urinate by wiping gently on the genitalia. Few queens can resist giving what we call "Tidy Didy Service," and once she washes the kitten she almost always accepts it.

Daily Weighing

The kittens should be weighed every day, preferably at the same time, and records of the weights kept. (Renew the color marking as necessary.) After all the kittens are born, I set up a page for their daily weights:

Kitten	#1	#2	#3	#4
Code	red, right	red, left	blue, right	blue, left
Birth	3.25	3.00	2.75	3.00
Day 1				
Day 2				
etc.				

Supplementation

If the queen continues to reject the kittens, remains dry, has too many to feed adequately, or one or more kittens is losing out to stronger sib-

Hand-feeding kittens. The medicine dropper or the Catac nurser can be used.

lings, it's time to get out the synthetic cat's milk and a feeder. These milks are the closest available to natural cat's milk and are different from those of dog and cow. If you cannot obtain them, you can use undiluted, canned evaporated cow's milk to which is added white corn syrup in the proportion of approximately 1 tablespoon of syrup per cup of milk, warmed to body temperature.

If you use a medicine dropper to feed the newborn, be sure to put just a drop at a time in its mouth until it catches on, literally, at which point it will quickly suck the milk out of the dropper. Give it as many droppersful as it wants; when it is full it will stop sucking. Never force milk down a kitten's throat; if the milk gets into the lungs, the kitten will die. When it is hungry again, in about three hours, it will cry for more. The Catac nurser and the Ipevet bottle with the smallest nipple are suitable for feeding kittens. The nipples are the size and shape of the queen's. There are nursers available that look like doll bottles. Do not waste your money on them. They are totally unsuited to Siamese kittens as the nipples are the wrong size and shape and there is no way to control the flow.

Whatever is used to handfeed, all parts of it must be washed with hot water and soap and rinsed thoroughly after each use. Milk residue is a perfect growth medium for bacteria. The milk substitute should be kept refrigerated and not used beyond 24 hours from the time of opening the can.

Weight Loss

It is common for a kitten to lose a fraction of an ounce between birth and the first day, but by the second day it should be gaining. Thereafter, a day without gain may happen, but a loss of weight or no gain for two days in succession is cause for concern. Immediate antibiotic therapy can save the kitten if it is in the early stages of peritonitis. Do not depend on some external sign to diagnose peritonitis; sometimes there is a pink ring at the base of the umbilicus (navel), but I have rarely seen it among my own fading kittens that have responded to antibiotic treatment.

If all of the above seems forbidding, that was my intention. A prospective breeder needs to know what can go wrong. On the other hand, sometimes everything goes right, and none of the information above is needed. Near the end of another pregnancy, our Raisinette showed no signs of imminent labor, other than dragging someone else's four-month-old kitten to bed with her in the wingback chair as we said goodnight. The next morning I went downstairs and headed for the kitchen, greeting Rai as I passed her, still in the chair in the living room—and then I did a classic double take. There were six babies with her, all clean and nursing, plus the older kitten, looking more confused than ever.

The First Week

Spotting

During the first week the queen may continue to "spot" dark blood. Do not be in a rush to change her bedding. A few dry bloodstains are not harmful. If it bothers you, just put another layer of bedding on top of the soiled one. That way the cat's odor is not suddenly removed from the box. In a day or two, when the uppermost bedding has taken on their odor, slip the older bedding out from under and wash it. Replacing all the bedding at once is upsetting to the kittens, as they are depending primarily on their sense of smell at this time.

Behavior

In the first week the kittens will nurse and sleep and occasionally fight over a nipple. When Mom takes a break, they pile on top of each other in a heap; sometimes she pulls a layer of bedding on top of them before she leaves. They creep around only to search for a nipple or a comfortable place to nap.

From the first day, monitor their health not only by daily weight but by behavior. Besides having full bellies and a firm feel to them, healthy kittens stay close to the queen and, when the queen is out of the box, to each other. A kitten off to the side, not nursing, slack-bodied, and cooler than the others is sick. If only one acts this way, take it to the veterinarian for evaluation. Usually, not much can be determined at this early age, but even without a conclusive diagnosis, antibiotic treatment is usually recommended. It may save the kitten, which has been my experience in the majority of cases; otherwise, the kitten is certain to die. If several or all of the kittens seem affected, take queen and kits to the veterinarian. If the queen goes into a heat cycle, her milk can carry enough hormones to be harmful to the kittens. Another possibility is a uterine infection that is producing toxins that get into the queen's circulation and from there into the milk. In either case, the kittens must be taken off the queen's milk until she is out of heat or the infection eliminated. If possible, find a foster mother for the kittens. Unfortunately, that is easier said than done. You will probably have to hand-feed the kittens until the queen is back to normal. In the first week, this means every three or four hours around the clock. If the kittens do not nurse on the queen for several days, she may dry up. To prevent this and to relieve the pressure in her breasts, milk a few drops from each breast by gently pinching the nipples and the area just around them several times a day. So that she maintains her bond with the kittens, let them visit her after you have fed them. If she is not ill, she will take this opportunity to wash them, especially the genitalia and anal area, which stimulates urination and defecation. If the queen cannot perform this duty, you must. Rub gently over the area with a small pad of tissue or a cotton ball moistened with warm water and, when the kitten is done, clean well with water and dry the area.

Handling

Whether the kittens are well or ill, they should be handled daily from the time they are born. Take ordinary precautions against infecting them: Don't sneeze or cough over them and wash your hands with plain soap to cut down on the germs you carry. (The object is to have the kittens smell you frequently as they feel you stroking them, so don't confuse them with strongly scented soap.) Talk to them every time you go to the box to check on them; use a soft, high-pitched tone in speaking to them in imitation of the queen's voice. These early contacts allow them to bond with a human and, in my opinion, are the foundation for very trusting relationships with you and other humans in the future.

Another advantage of handling the kittens is to transmit a few ordinary, not pathogenic ("household") bacteria to them and to the queen, whose already-developed immune system will make antibodies to the bacteria. Research has shown that kittens' immune systems need some challenges in order to develop properly. Trying to keep kittens in a sterile environment will result in a deficient immune system—a serious mistake.

Color

Near the end of the first week the very first color begins to show in the new hairs growing along the edges of the ears, their coolest area. Seal and blue points usually color in first, followed by chocolate point, and last, lilac point. In the second week the fur on the tail will take on a tinge of color, although it will still be difficult to be certain of the point color, if more than one is genetically possible. Color

begins to come on the tip of the nose, too. Even so, it might be weeks more before you are certain of the color.

The Second Week

Some time during the second week the kittens should double their birth weight. If they do not, yet seem well, it may be that there is not enough milk for them or that the milk is somehow deficient. Again, get out the synthetic cat's milk or undiluted evaporated milk and supplement their diet.

Eyes

Also in the second week their eyes should open. Again, there is variability both from litter to litter and within a litter. Among my litters it has ranged from five to twelve days, and within a litter, one to three days. Exactly when is not so important as watching for infections from the moment the eyes begin to open. Bacteria may be washed into the tiniest first opening by the queen's tongue as she grooms them. This can lead to an infection behind the still mostly closed eyelids. One must not try to force open the eyelids, but if the eyes seem to be bulging more than in the first few days or you detect the smallest crust or ooze along the juncture of the eyelids, immediate action is called for. Soak the area with warm (human) eyewash or sterile saline solution. If there is pus behind the eyelids, it can glue up the edges that should be turning loose. If this is the case, the soaking will unglue the lids and allow them to open, releasing the built-up pus. Antibiotic ointment or drops will surely be prescribed by your veterinarian. Infections at this stage are common; most are cleared up within a few days. *But* they should always be taken very seriously, as they can lead to corneal ulceration, rupture of the eye, or, at worst, blindness and months of treatments with many different, very expensive medications that have to be given frequently and not at the same times.

Breeding

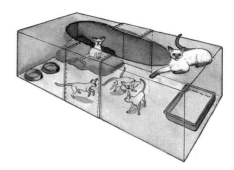

A playpen made from two corrugated boxes.

A multi-level cage playpen.

The Third Week

During the third week the kittens should start moving around more in the nest box. Now is the time to get them a playpen. There are excellent cages for cats that are suitable as playpens; they are taller than wide, have several perches, and two doors—one halfway up and the other at the bottom. The floor area is large enough for the nest box or a bed, a small litter box, and food and water dishes. However, a fine playpen can be made from two large cardboard boxes of the size that contain paper towels. Put them on their sides, opening to opening, with flaps extended and overlapping. With a carpet needle and either dental floss or heavy-duty thread sew the overlapping flaps together. Next, draw an oval on the upper surface of the conjoined boxes, leaving enough of an edge to support the queen. Cut along the oval with a serrated knife and the playpen is made. There is plenty of room for a bed, a small litter box, toys, and scampering. The queen can jump in and out easily or sit on the rim and watch the babies at play. It is very important that, as the kittens

get older, the queen be allowed to get away from them whenever she wishes; otherwise, she can be driven to harming the kittens.

The Fourth Week and Beyond

By the fourth week the kittens will begin exploring and trying to climb out of the nest box. The scritch-scratch of their little nails on the walls of the box and the first little face peering out of the semicircular opening signal time for transfer to the playpen. If the playpen is the cage, hang one of the perches level with the upper door, which should be left open for the queen, and close the lower door. The nest box may be put in or else just the bedding from it. Unless the room is very warm and draft-free, drape a sheet around the top and three sides of the cage. I place a stool or small chair alongside the open cage door to assist the queen in reentering the cage. If the playpen is the homemade rig, the drape and chair are not needed.

Above left: Outdoor life will produce a heavier and fluffier ▶ coat, as shown by this blue point.
Above right: Siamese are inquisitive to a fault and must be kept away from poisonous plants.
Below: All Siamese enjoy playing at attack.

Breeding

Beginning to Wean

By the fourth week you may also notice that the queen leaves the nest more frequently and stays away for longer periods. This is the result of the normal decline in hormones that promote mothering and coincides with the beginning of the weaning process. Some kittens are ready to start eating at this point, but Siamese may not be, although their first teeth are coming in. One way to test their readiness is to offer them some very smoothly prepared meat, such as strained chicken baby food. Even when they begin to eat, they should not be taken from the mother. Over a period of three weeks or so they should gradually shift from only nursing to nursing and eating to, finally, only eating. Of course, during this time they should also be provided with water (in a nontippable bowl) and their first litter pan.

Kitten Foods

Once the kittens begin to eat solid food, do not give them milk, even if they were being supplemented earlier. Most Siamese lose the ability to digest lactose as they mature and get diarrhea if they continue to drink it. The calcium and other nutrients that a kitten needs are found in the kitten formulas of prepared foods that specify that they are 100% nutritionally complete. This is what they should be fed once they have mastered eating baby food. Good quality kitten foods come in both wet (canned) preparations and dry (we call them baby rocks). The semi-moist preparations are not recommended for cats or kittens because of the propylene glycol content, which may not be listed on the label.

◀ Siamese make excellent companions to children and adults.

The dry kitten food can be given as soon as their teeth are in. Some take to it dry right away; others prefer it moistened with water. Whatever the type of food, let them have as much as they want. For wet food, this means four or five meals a day. Dry food can be left in a dish, as it does not spoil at room temperature.

Litter Pans

The first litter pan should be shallow enough to allow easy access. There are small plastic pans that are suitable or the lid of a shoe box will do. Do not start them out with regular litter; they try to eat it. If they ingest too much, there is a danger of bowel obstruction. Instead, begin with a pad of paper toweling covered with shredded paper (towels, tissues, or newspaper). Contrary to popular belief, the queen does not teach them to use the litter, although she may drag them into the pan. This behavior is an instinct that is switched on during the weaning period, and urinating in the pan may occur even before the kitten begins to eat.

Being Careful

The next two or three weeks are the most trying and the most entertaining for the breeder. Watching the kittens beginning to play with each other and with the simple toys you put in their playpen and seeing the day-to-day changes in them is more fun than a circus. You may want to take them out to love them and let them scamper about the room, but do not leave them unattended. Invariably, they look for electrical cords to chew on, and, should Nature call, they "go" wherever they are. Do not expect them to be able to get back to the litter pan on their own at this age. Even while in the playpen and near the litter pan, they will have accidents, which they usually walk through and track all over the bedding. So be prepared for frequent changes of bedding and kitten cleanups. (Once they start eating a significant amount of solid food, the queen cancels the Tidy Didy Service.) When their motor skills catch up with their toilet instincts these problems disappear.

The proper way to hold a kitten or cat. The paws are controlled and the weight is supported.

All they will need is a not-too-distant and clean toilet, to which you can begin adding regular litter.

There are two cautions about handling kittens: Never pick them up by the scruff of the neck and never roughhouse with them. If the kitten is too big to fit in your hand, put one hand under its chest, with your forefinger directed forward between its arms and your thumb and remaining fingers curving up around either side and behind the arms; place your other hand under its hindquarters. Suspending a kitten by its neck skin can cause serious nerve damage and paralysis. The queen may drag them around the box by the nape, but when she wants to travel, she picks one up by the whole neck, which fits without harm across her partially closed mouth in the gap between her canines and premolars.

Time to Advertise

At the end of the first month, the kittens begin to look like little Siamese instead of white mice. Some breeders advertise at this time and allow serious prospective buyers to see the kittens and to make reservations if all is satisfactory.

Socialization

During the second month kittens begin to play very roughly with each other and are happy to accept a human hand as another rowdy playmate. Do not be tempted. Kitten skin is tougher and better protected than human skin. More importantly, kittens that are taught to play rough with humans will grow into cats that cannot be petted without the danger of a painful play attack. Make it a firm rule that all direct contacts with the kittens are of a soothing, gentle nature. When you want to play with the kittens, do so with an extension of yourself, such as a yarn "spider" or a twist of paper on a string. When the kittens become good runners, throw a small sponge ball or a piece of crumpled-up paper. They love to chase these imitation mice and may surprise you by initiating a game of fetch.

Scratching Material

By now, the kittens are about seven weeks old and very active. Give them as much time out of the nursery cage or box as possible, or provide a kitten-safe room for them. Provide a scrap of carpeting for them that is at least one foot wide and two feet long. If you get the kind that has a jute backing, lay the scrap face down so that the jute side is uppermost. If not, choose a tight, nubby weave and place it right side up. They will scratch like grownups on these materials.

Final Weaning

When they have been eating mostly solid food for at least a week, with occasional milk meals from the queen, it is time to begin planning their weaning. This is painful for all concerned, but necessary. However, sooner is *not* better than later. Kittens that are weaned too early may fail to thrive or even become ill. They may also grow up with the need to suck, which can be a nuisance when they suck or chew on substances such as your best sweater. Let the queen's attitude toward them and the kittens' condition be your guide.

Scratching material. The jute backing is often more inviting to the cat than the "right" side.

If she gets up and leaves while they are nursing or otherwise shows impatience, the time is soon. If the kittens are healthy, gaining weight steadily, and have been eating solid food for at least two weeks, they are ready for weaning.

The painful part is keeping the queen and kittens apart. The queen's breasts become engorged with milk soon after they are separated. It is best to keep her in a different room altogether. Gradually milk production will stop and the swelling will subside. She can then return to the kittens' room, but must not let them nurse again. If she does not fend off their attempts to nurse, they cannot be left together.

Vaccinations

Now is the time to think also of vaccinations. Some breeders have the kittens vaccinated with the "three-in-one" vaccine against rhinotracheitis, calici, and feline panleukopenia viruses three times—at about six weeks, at one week after weaning is complete, and, finally, two to three weeks later. I prefer twice, waiting until one week after weaning to give the first vaccination. Although it is not certain to what extent the antibodies in the queen's milk get across the kitten's intestine and into its blood, my practice has been to wait one week after their last feeding on the queen before having them vaccinated for the first time. This allows whatever antibodies may have entered from the milk to disappear and not interfere with the challenge to the immune system by the vaccine. Two weeks later they get the second vaccination. With both sequences the production of their own antibodies is raised to a level that will protect them for a year, at which time they should receive a booster.

Types of Vaccinations

There are various combinations of vaccines that are given to kittens. The three-in-one vaccine is considered safe for kittens at the weaning stage. The four-in-one, which contains, in addition, anti-chlamydia vaccine, is not recommended for kittens younger than nine weeks. Kittens should have rabies vaccine and leukemia vaccine at some point. Whether they receive them before or after they go to their new homes will depend on timing and your budget. At the very least, they should have received a three-in-one vaccination in the tenth to fourteenth week. Consult your veterinarian for what is best for your kittens.

Method

For any injections, but particularly the first vaccination, the two-needle method is preferred. After withdrawing the vaccine from the vial and before injecting the kitten, the veterinarian changes to a fresh needle. This provides the sharpest possible needle point for the injection, making it as painless as possible. More importantly for vaccines, it provides a needle that has no vaccine on it as it enters the kitten's skin. The first needle has been in the vaccine and could leave some on the surface of the skin and fur if it were used to inject.

If the kitten were to lick that area, which they usually do, there is a distinct possibility of acquiring the disease against which it is being vaccinated. Many vaccines contain live, attenuated (weakened) viruses. For some of these viruses the natural tissue of infection is the digestive tract. If the kitten ingests these viruses shortly after inoculation, there is a real chance of an infection, with vomiting and diarrhea, which can lead to dehydration and death if not treated promptly.

Registration

By now, the kittens are two months or older, depending on how early they were weaned. Their point colors and sexes should be evident, so it is time to register them. If you have not already registered a cattery name and plan to continue breeding, you may want to do so now. Your cattery name will be the first name, automatically, of all kittens born to your females and registered with that association.

How to Register

There are two stages of kitten registration: litter registration and individual registration. Special litter registration forms are available without charge from each of the registries. The litter as a unit must be registered first. This is done by completing the form with the appropriate information, such as birth date of the litter, names and registration numbers of the dam and sire, and signatures of the breeder (owner of the dam) and owner of the sire. If you do not own the sire, you must fill out the form and send it to the sire's owner to be signed and returned to you. There is space on the litter registration form for individual registration of any or all of the kittens. This is usually done only if the breeder plans to keep one or more of the litter. A small fee is charged to register the litter; to register individuals carries an additional fee. Upon receipt of the litter registration form and fee, the registry will send you a separate slip for each kitten. This slip is to be completed by

the new owner of the kitten and sent back to the registry with the individual registration fee. Finally, the registry will send the individual registration.

Planning for the Kittens' Departure

This brings us to planning for the kittens' departure. The only thing that eases the pain of seeing them go is knowing that they are going to good homes. So the primary task is to find prospective buyers and to screen them carefully. And we have come full circle—from how to find a Siamese kitten to how to place one.

Finding Buyers

Finding prospective buyers, especially for the new breeder, may require a shotgun approach. Newspapers are a good place to start; some have weekend specials, which are lower than the daily rate and are published when most people look for kitten ads. (Do not include your home address.) Ask your veterinarian if you can place a notice on the clinic bulletin board. Community bulletin boards at libraries, schools, supermarkets, etc., are other possibilities. Cat magazines are another good source, but the ad must be submitted well in advance of the time the kittens will be available. And, of course, word of mouth. Take photos of the little darlings with you wherever you go, and don't hesitate to whip them out at the mention of anything remotely related to felines.

Screening Callers

Before the telephone calls begin to come in, make up a list of things that you will want to know about the caller and what you think the serious caller will want to know about the kittens. Include, of course, the price of the kitten sold as a pet (to be altered) and that of a breeder or show-quality kitten (altering not required), what vaccinations they have had, and what guarantees you offer. (An unconditional guarantee for one week with full refund of the purchase price is the best insurance you can have that, should the kitten not be a good match to the buyer, you will get the kitten back quickly and in good condition.) You will want to know whether the caller has had a cat before, and why the caller wants a Siamese kitten. If the caller recently lost a kitten or cat, ask the cause of death. Try to determine what sort of value the caller places on a pet, as compared to inanimate objects. Unless the caller sounds legitimate and makes a definite appointment to see the kittens, do not give your home address.

Visitations

When prospective buyers come, it is best to have the kittens in their usual location. If the kittens live in your bedroom, show them there. If you bring the kittens to a strange room, they will not be at their best, either running around like crazy in the new territory or hiding under the sofa.

The Kitten's Kit

Before the departure date of a kitten, make up a packet to accompany it to its new home. Some of the items to include are:
• litter registration slip
• vaccination records
• a piece of used bedding
• a small plastic bag of lightly soiled litter
• a scrap of carpeting
• feeding instructions
• a jar of baby food

• a tube of low-volume, high-calorie supplement
• your name, address, and telephone number
• your veterinarian's name, address, and telephone number

Using a Carrier

Be sure to tell prospective buyers that a proper carrier is required. My rule is "No carrier, no kitten." Impress upon the buyer the many dangers of opening the carrier in transit and of leaving the kitten alone in the car, even for just a few minutes. The carrier should not be opened until it is safely inside the kitten's new home with all outside doors closed and open windows fully screened. Behind these warnings are many horror stories best left untold.

The Guarantee

As the kitten leaves with its new owners, I remind them that, should the kitten not suit them for any reason whatsoever, I want it back. I also urge them to call me at any time if they have a question or concern about the kitten. Finally, I tell them that should some unforeseen circumstance, no matter how far in the future, require that they give up the cat, I will always take it back and find a home for it.

As you can see from all of the above, the person who breeds Siamese is not likely to make a monetary profit. Having the kittens for a time and making new and very special friends through them is the profit.

Grooming

The healthy Siamese requires little in the way of grooming. However, that little is important and should best be done with as little fuss as possible.

Head

Eyes

Starting at the front, the eyes may become irritated by smoke or allergens, resulting in the production of mucus, which dries in the corners of the eyes. These dried secretions can be removed with a tissue, but you may have to immobilize the cat to do so. Cats hate having anything done to their eyes. My method is to kneel on the floor with the cat facing outward between my knees; then, one hand can hold the head and pull down on the lower eyelid while the other wields the tissue or applies eye drops or ointment.

Ears

Next, the ears. Ears, even when healthy, need to be cleaned from time to time. How often varies from cat to cat. If brown secretions are visible in the ears, arm yourself with many cotton swabs and clean away. Do not be afraid of damaging the ear drum; the cat's ear canal is U-shaped. So, swab away without fear.

Chin

On Siamese the chin seems particularly susceptible to a condition known as chin acne. This has been described earlier, on page 33. The best preventative for this is a clean chin. If your Siamese is lax in washing its chin, scrub its chin with plain soap and water and rinse well.

Teeth and Gums

Some Siamese, as they get older, develop gum disease. Brushing their teeth may help prevent this by removing plaque before it hardens into tartar. This is definitely one of those things that is easier said than done. There are various techniques, but the ones I have found easiest to manage are a dry,

cotton-tipped swab or a fingertip with a two-inch-square scrap of thin terrycloth. The best I can do is the outer surfaces, but I have heard of cats that also allow the inner surfaces to be done. Do not use toothpaste for humans as some of it contains compounds that are dangerous to cats, and trying to rinse a cat's mouth after brushing really makes the whole experience burdensome, if not impossible.

Nails

Nails must be clipped every two to three weeks. Even with scratching posts to help pull off the old, outer sheaths of nail, further help in the form of clipping is needed. Pick a time when the Siamese is dozing. Gently press on the top of each toe to cause the nail to extend. Using a nail clipper or cat nail scissors, clip off the white portion of each nail.

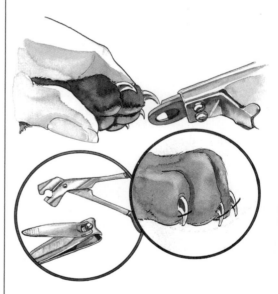

Clipping nails. Gently compress palm and knuckles to extend the claw. Cut below the quick using guillotine cutter, cat claw scissors, or nail clippers.

Stay away from the pink area; that is the "quick." Some Siamese are very tolerant of this procedure. If yours is not, you may need to enlist a pedicure partner. While you wield the clippers, have the partner pinch the neck skin of the Siamese, without pulling upward. This evokes the "freeze" response of kittenhood and gives you more wiggle-free time to do the job.

Coat

Bathing a Siamese should not be a regular occurrence. The only times I have ever bathed my Siamese are when they picked up some fleas or got into dirty mischief. I still see this picture: I open the basement door and up comes this *blue* cat. How did a stray blue cat get into my basement? Wait, it has blue eyes; it's not a stray. It's our formerly gorgeous lilac-point Phussati, she of the Merry Widow genes, all over blue with soot. Words cannot express my trepidation at the thought of bathing that particular Siamese.

Bathing

There are three basic ways to bathe a cat: the bucket method, the birdbath, and the shower. The trick is in discovering which is least frightening to your Siamese and thus the safest and easiest for all concerned. Whichever method you use, prepare everything—the room, the water, yourself—before bringing in the cat, whose nails were clipped the day before.

The room should be warm, draft-free, and wet-scared-catproof. Bathrooms are ideal. Remove all breakables. Loop shower and window curtains out of the way. Put out a face cloth, at least two bath towels, cat shampoo (mild, unscented hand-dishwashing liquid is good), and a bathmat or rug on which to kneel.

The water should be the temperature of the cat's body, which is about 102°F (39°C). If you use a thermometer to check the water temperature, be sure to put it away before bringing in the Siamese.

Prepare yourself physically by removing all jewelry and wearing old, tough clothes. Mental preparation involves repeating to yourself a few hundred times, "I will be calm and determined, and all will go well."

Bucket Method

The bucket method calls for two, preferably three buckets, pails, or plastic wastebaskets. Rectangular ones fit better side by side in the bathtub than round ones. Fill each bucket with cat-temperature water to within three or four inches of the top. If you overfill them, the sound of the water spilling out as you put the cat in can be the last straw for an apprehensive cat. To the first bucket add a tablespoon of cat shampoo or the mild hand-dishwashing liquid, and mix. This will aid in wetting the cat's fur. The second and third buckets are for rinsing. Now you bring in the bathee. If fleas are suspected, wet the cat's neck all around with the shampoo and work it in well before you start the bath. This keeps the fleas from going up to hide in the ears and facial fur when the rest of the cat is

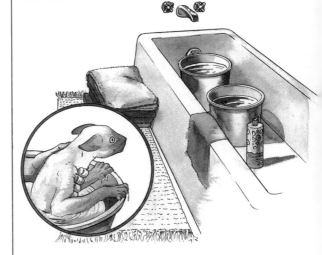

The two-bucket method of bathing. Be sure to have plenty of towels nearby.

immersed. Hold the cat firmly as described before, one hand under the chest with a grip between and behind the arms and the other under the rump. Lower the cat slowly into the soapy water. Avoid splashing, which frightens most cats. The cat will probably grip the edge of the bucket, but will not be terribly upset with being in water if the water is at its body temperature and its face does not get splashed. Maintain the chest-arm grip and use the other hand to go through its fur, making sure that the water penetrates it. Lift the cat out, set it down in the tub, pour on more shampoo and work it into the coat, keeping that chest grip all the while. When the cleansing is done, immerse the cat in the first bucket once more, making sure to wet the neck well. This serves as a first rinse. Take the cat out and squeegee it with your free hand, going from the neck along the back to the end of the tail and down each leg. Repeat this rinsing and squeegeeing process through the second and third buckets.

Birdbath Method

The second method, the birdbath, is a modification of the bucket method. Instead of buckets, shallow containers, such as dishpans, are used. Again, rectangular ones work best. Cats that cannot be put into water up to their necks in buckets may be willing to stand in a few inches of water in a pan. The sequence is the same for the bucket method, but getting the coat wet and clean all over is harder. A face cloth helps and is less splashy than scooping up water by hand to wet the cat.

Shower Method

The shower method requires a hand-held spray attachment for the bathtub faucet or the use of the kitchen sink, if it has a built-in sprayer. The water temperature must be adjusted carefully in advance and left turned on to a gentle spray. If the sprayer is held right against a cat's body it does not seem to frighten them. The sequence again is the same—wet, shampoo, rinse thoroughly, and squeegee off the excess water.

You may find that some combination of these methods works best for you and your Siamese. For example, you may be able to immerse it once, but there is no way it is going back into all that wet stuff up to its neck. In this case, a birdbath or shower finish will be considered not so bad and better tolerated.

After the last squeegeeing, wrap the cat in a towel with only its head out and hold it on your lap. Clean the ears with cotton-tipped swabs. If the face needs washing, use the corner of the face cloth. Be careful to avoid getting shampoo in its eyes. When the towel feels damp, change to a second one. Rub the fur every which way to further dry it. If necessary, use a third towel. Empty the buckets, wipe up the drips and spills, make a dry bed for the damp, mad Siamese, and leave it in the bathroom to rewash and dry itself (with its own little pink washcloth), while you prepare a special dinner for it. An extra serving of the offended one's favorite food soothes its nerves and mends the snag in the feline-human friendship.

As you can see, I am a firm believer in preparing for the worst while hoping for the best. You may be wondering how I fared with blue Phussati. Much to my surprise, it was the easiest cat bath I ever gave. She was scared enough to go into a catatonic trance, but not so scared that she became panicky. It was like washing a doll.

Combing and Brushing

A more common and less traumatic form of coat grooming is simply combing or brushing, with none of that wet stuff around. A pocket comb will do for clearing the coat of loose hairs; simply comb with the direction of hair growth—from head to tail. Most cats enjoy this. Slightly damp hands can accomplish the same thing, but you must first rub the fur backward, from tail to head, and then head to tail.

For special purposes, special grooming aids are called for. There are many pet combs and brushes available. Do not use wire brushes on Siamese; they are designed for the heavier coats and larger bodies of dogs. If you suspect your Siamese has fleas, there are small, metal flea combs that can be used on cats and that are effective in capturing fleas. Use short strokes in the direction of hair growth, and, when the fleas are caught, dunk the comb into a bowl of soapy water where the fleas will come out of the comb and be drowned.

Human hairbrushes will not do much for a cat's coat, but there are solid rubber brushes for cats that will. These are about the size and shape of a nail brush. One side of the brush has a flat bed of hundreds of quarter-inch-long, finger like projections. This side is used to clear loose hairs from the coat by ordinary brushing strokes from head to tail. My Siamese line up for this and never seem to get enough of it. The base of the other side of the brush is cut into a shallow V and covered with shorter projections. This side is used with a short, scooping motion—again, in the direction of hair growth, and will remove not only loose hairs but some that are not. The effect is to thin the coat, but excessive use could make scanty or bald spots in the coat.

Tail

And finally, we come to the end of the cat and the one place the Siamese most welcomes grooming assistance—its tail tip. It seems that tail tips are difficult to wash, perhaps because they are at the end of those long, flexible tails and can be washed in one direction only—tipward. Years ago I discovered that if you hold the tail about one inch from the tip and present it to the Siamese it will scrub it vigorously in every direction (as they do their body fur), happily leaving it a bushy, but clean mess!

Showing Your Siamese

Showing your Siamese can be fun and very educational, but it is not for everyone nor for every Siamese. Before deciding about showing your Siamese, it would be wise to visit a show or two and watch the goings-on. You will see a certain tension as the exhibitors (owners) take their cats to each of the judging areas, wait while their cat is judged, and then wait again to see if the cat is called back for the finals. Even the best cats do not make the top five in every final, so some disappointment is a given. But for those who do not expect to place in every final and who enjoy the many other aspects of showing, the pleasures outweigh the pains.

Qualifications

Once you decide that you want to show your Siamese, you must familiarize yourself with the qualities expected of a show Siamese and determine whether yours is eligible to be shown. The first requirement is that your Siamese be registered or, at least, have registered parents.

Breed Standards

If your Siamese came from a breeder, ask the breeder to evaluate the show potential of your cat. Even if your Siamese is a kitten, the experienced breeder should be able to tell you whether it is likely to be show quality. Other valuable sources of information are the breed standards and show rules of the various cat registries (see Useful Literature and Addresses). These cost only a few dollars and provide a wealth of information. The show rules describe the format of the shows sanctioned by that registry, the eligibility rules, the judging procedures, and much more. The breed standards include descriptions of every breed, including Siamese, of course, recognized by that organization. The Siamese breed standard will describe the ideal Siamese and the point allotment for each feature of the cat. The total number of points for the ideal is 100, but even the winningest Siamese may be a point or two shy of perfection.

General Guidelines

Disqualifications

If you must evaluate your cat without assistance, here are some general guidelines. First, there are grounds for disqualification that apply to all breeds. Most of these are for physical conditions, including blindness, malocclusion, pregnancy, cryptorchidism (testicles not descended), an abnormal number of toes, and a lack of claws, but unruly behavior can also be a cause for disqualification if the cat cannot be handled by the judge even with the assistance of the owner. Altered (castrated, spayed) cats may be shown, but compete in their own division.

Faults

Then there are faults that are described for each breed. In the Siamese breed there are certain traits that are considered so undesirable that most organizations require that all wins be withheld (W/W) if the cat or kitten has any one of these: crossed eye, kinked tail, white spot, or eye color other than blue.

Condition

Finally, the ultimate test of your cat's show potential is the show ring itself. If your Siamese is registered or registerable, has none of the major faults above, is not excessively shy or frightened of strangers, and you want to give showing a try, enter a show and see what happens. But before you do anything else, be sure that your Siamese is eating a healthful diet (see the chapter on nutrition, if in doubt), is free of internal and external parasites, and has no health problems. These things are absolute necessities for good general condition and a chance at winning in shows. Improving your cat's condition to show standards may take weeks, if it is overweight, for example, or months, if a deficient diet or disease has given it a rough, coarse coat.

Finding a Show

The next step is to locate shows in your area. Check the show calendars in the cat magazines and contact the cat registries. The registries may also give you a list of their clubs in your area, as individual clubs are usually the sponsors of the shows. Once you have found a show that is in your area, check the entry deadline. Shows usually close entries about one month before the date of the show. If the deadline is just past, call the entry clerk; there may be a chance of getting your entry in. If time is no problem, write or call the entry clerk for an entry blank and a show flyer, which gives basic information about the show. Be sure to indicate that you are a new exhibitor, as many clubs will provide extra information in advance and special assistance at the show.

Entering

The entry blank will look something like the following:

Cat's Name	Color		Sex
Registration Number	Breed	Eye Color	Birthdate
Sire's Name		Registration number, if required	
Dam's Name		Registration number, if required	
Breeder		Agent	
Owner's Name		Telephone Number	
Owner' Address			

Competition Class

Household Pet		Nonchampionship
__ LH	__ SH	__ Kitten
__ Kitten	__ Adult	__ AOV
		__ Experimental Breed

Alter (Premier) Division	Championship Division
__ Novice	__ Novice
__ Champion (Premier)	__ Champion
__ Grand Champion (Premier)	__ Grand Champion

Special Benching Requests:

The first several lines call for information that is on the cat's individual registration certificate. If your Siamese is registered with an association other than the one sanctioning the show, you will have to either register it with the show's association or supply registration numbers (from any registry) for its sire and dam, plus a small "listing" fee.

An agent is someone authorized to show the cat for you and need be designated only if you are not attending the show yourself. Sometimes exhibitors put in a fellow exhibitor's name just to be covered in case they have to leave the show hall for a time.

The competition class can be confusing to the beginner. If your Siamese cannot be registered or for some other reason is ineligible for showing as a pedigreed cat, it could be shown as a household pet. In that case, under Household Pet you would check the SH for shorthair, and either Kitten, if it will be at least four months old but not yet eight months old on the day of the show, or Adult, if it will be eight months or older then.

Most Siamese fit into one of the other categories. If your Siamese is eligible for show and will be at least four months old but not yet eight months old on the day of the show, check the Kitten blank under Nonchampionship. If the eligible Siamese will be eight months or older on the day of the show, has not earned a championship in show already, and is whole (not castrated or spayed), check the Novice space under Championship Division, or, if it has been castrated or spayed, the Novice space under Alter (Premier) Division.

If you have a Siamese that was already shown to champion or grand champion and the title was "claimed" (validated), it should be entered as a Champion or a Grand. If it earned a title as a whole cat and then was altered, it must enter as an Alter (Premier) Novice.

Benching refers to the cage position assigned to your cat in the show hall. If your cat is being agented, but sure to write that your entry must be benched with (name of agent). A physically disabled person might ask to be benched at the end of a row and near the judging rings. Frequently, friends ask to be benched together so that they can help each other and socialize in between judgings. As a new exhibitor, you could ask to be benched next to a club member or some other experienced exhibitor who would be willing to answer questions and show you the ropes.

The entry fee is given in the show calendar listing and on the show flyer. The fees vary, as they are based on the number of judging rings, which can be four to six in a one-day show and even more in a two- or three-day show. On the average, the range is $35 to $65. The fee must be sent (as a check or money order) with the completed and signed entry form to the entry clerk.

Confirmation

A confirmation of your entry will be sent to you shortly after the entry clerk receives the form and fee. If you do not receive a confirmation within two weeks, telephone the clerk. With the confirmation there will be further information about the show, including travel directions and the dimensions of the cages.

Grooming

Grooming of your Siamese is minimal. Unless they escape into the basement and get filthy, they need not be bathed. In fact, bathing will remove the natural oils in the coat and make it fluffy, which is highly undesirable. The nails on all the feet should be clipped. Some exhibitors trim the "ear furnishings"—the hair inside the ears—to enhance the size of the ears. A rubber brush is useful in removing loose hairs. A chamois cloth smoothed over the coat helps remove static electricity and flatten the coat.

A Day at a Show

But before we get into the details of preparation for the show, let us take a quick walk-through of a show day.

Check-in time is given on the confirmation sheet as 8:00–9:00 am. You and Sammi (in her carrier)

On the judging table at a cat show.

arrive at the show hall at 8:15 am. Just inside is the entry clerk, who checks you and Sammi in and either gives or sells you a show catalog (an absolute must). The clerk or another official will direct you to your cage among 200 or so cages, usually arranged in double rows. On her cage will be a card with her entry number, let's say it is #132. You put Sammi, still in her carrier, under her cage while you hang her cage drapes, put a mat and small bed on its floor, obtain a disposable pan with litter (usually provided by the show), and half fill her water dish. Now Sammi gets transferred from her carrier to her cage. She will probably be nervous. Pull up a chair and say sweet nothings to her while you quickly check out the competition in the show catalog. Turning to the page where Sammi is listed, you see that there is another lilac-point female novice, #133, who will be in direct competition with Sammi, as well as a lilac-point male novice, #131, and a lilac-point female grand champion, #134. So there will be four lilac points competing for the best of color in their color class.

On the back of the catalog will be a show schedule. Each judging ring is listed, with the order

76

of judging under it. Circle Sammi's group—Championship, Siamese—for each ring so that you will be able to tell at a glance where she will be called for judging throughout the day.

If Sammi has settled, take a walk around and see if you can spot cage #133. There she is. Hmmmm. Her coat is nice and flat, but her ears are too small, and is that a little scratch on her nose? Check on Sammi, and, if time permits, the other lilac points. By now, the show should be getting underway. Check-in time is over, and the entry clerk announces that he is ready to read the absentees and and transfers. When he gets to the Siamese numbers he says that #131 has been transferred to champion. Note this in the catalog. This means that since the lilac-point male novice was entered in this show he attended another show and made his championship. Number 134 is absent, so put an A in the catalog by her number.

When the clerk is done with the absentees and transfers, the ring clerks will begin calling for the first groups to be judged in their rings. Sammi is near the beginning of the schedule for Ring 3, Judge Gamma, so keep your ears perked for Ring 3 announcements. Time to check her eyes for cruds, smooth her coat with a chamois cloth, and give her a little treat, such as four licks of baby-food chicken. Then comes the fateful announcement, "Ring three wants the following cats: #131, #132, #133..." Put pen, catalog, and chamois in your pockets and holding Sammi close to you with both hands, carry her to Ring 3 and put her in the judging cage that has her number on it. Give her a gentle wipe with the chamois to settle her fur and your nerves, tell her not to be afraid, close the cage door, and find a seat in front of the judging table. The judge takes out one cat at a time, puts it on the table, scrutinizes it, returns it to its judging cage, writes in her book, and then may hang one or more ribbons on the front of the cage.

It's Sammi's turn. Will she behave? Will she let the judge stretch her out to see her body length? Will she cross her eyes? The suspense is indescribable.

The whole world disappears except Sammi and Judge Gamma until she is back in the cage. Whew! No mishaps, but did she like her? The ribbons will tell, but first #133 must be judged. Her ears are definitely too small, but did Judge Gamma note this? Ahhh, a blue ribbon for Sammi, and a Winner's ribbon, and a Best of Color! The clerk says they may go back. Honeybun! You were wonderful, you could make it to the finals! There are kisses and hugs for Sammi and another five licks of baby food at her cage.

At the end of the day, six or seven o'clock, Sammi has been through five rings, five judges, has won some and lost some, has had lots of licks of baby food, and it has been exhilarating. You gather up your ribbons and rosettes, put Sammi in her carrier, take down the cage drapes, and depart, a weary, happy, experienced exhibitor and Siamese.

Preparing for a Show

Materials

To prepare for a show requires some very down-to-earth information and an understanding of the ideal of the Siamese standard. The practical side includes making cage drapes of the correct dimensions (bath towels will do), arranging fasteners to hang them, fixing up a show kit of eye wash, cotton swabs, tissues, baby food, low-volume, high-calorie supplement as a treat, twist-ties or pipe cleaners to secure loose cage connections, and a favorite bed. A plastic cover for the top of the cage is useful in winter months.

Basis of Judging

These sorts of details are picked up readily. How the judges choose the best-of-breed Siamese and finalists takes a bit more study.

As a starting place, the following consensus of standards from five registries has been constructed. This is not a substitute for the individual Siamese standards of the various registries, which should be obtained and studied if you plan to show.

General Siamese Breed Standard

The ideal Siamese is a lithe, fine-boned cat of medium size with long, tapering lines. Males may be larger than females. The musculature is hard and sleek. Coat color is restricted to the points (face, ears, feet/legs, and tail); eye color is blue.

Part	Points	Description
Head	22	The head is a triangular wedge, with straight lines from a finely pointed muzzle along the sides to the outer base of the ears, which are large and set so that they continue the side lines of the head when viewed from the front. Bulging masseter muscles (stud jowls) are allowed in males. Seen from the side, there is a straight line from the tip of the nose to the top of the head and another straight line from the nose tip to the chin, which should be neither jutting out nor receding. The distance between the eyes is no less than the width of one eye.
Eyes	14	The eyes are almond-shaped and set at a slant toward the nose and in harmony with the side lines of the head. The color is a deep, vivid blue.
Body	30	The neck is long and slender. The body is long and tubular from the shoulders to the hips and is firmly muscled all over. The legs are long and fine-boned, with the hind legs longer than the front. The feet are small and oval. The tail is slender and tapering. The length should be equal to the length of the body or of the extended hind leg.
Coat	10	The coat is short, fine-textured, glossy, and close-lying.
Color	17	The points are evenly colored and matched, well defined, and contain no white or ticked hairs. The body color is a paler, even shade of the point color. Older cats are allowed to have darker body shading, but there must be a definite contrast between the body and points.
Condition and Balance	7	The cat appears hard, muscular, and bright-eyed. It is neither flabby, emaciated, nor fat. All of its parts should harmonize—for example, if the body is moderately long, the head should not be extremely long.
	100 points	

Serious faults: Paw pads or nose leather of wrong color for points; miniaturization; sanded or shaved coat; crossed eyes; visible tail vertebral defects; white toes or spots.

Books

Michael Wright and Sally Waters, eds. *The Book of the Cat.* New York: Summit Books, 1980.

Katrin Behrend and Monica Wegler, *The Complete Book of Cat Care.* New York: Barron's, 1991.

Jean Holzworth. *Diseases of the Cat.* Vol. 1. Philadelphia: W. B. Saunders Company, 1987.

Roy Robinson. *Genetics for Cat Breeders.* 2nd ed. Oxford: Pergamon Press, 1977.

Michael W. Fox. *Understanding Your Cat.* New York: Coward, McCann & Geoghegan, Inc., 1974.

Magazines

Cats	P.O. Box 290037 Port Orange, FL 32129-0037
Cat Fancy	P.O. Box 6050 Mission Viejo, CA 92690
I Love Cats	P.O. Box 7013 Red Oak, IA 51591-2013

Cat Registries

The American Cat Association, Inc.
8101 Katherine Avenue
Panorama City, CA 91402

American Cat Fanciers Association, Inc.
P.O. Box 203
Point Lookout, MO 65726

Canadian Cat Association
52 Dean Street
Brampton, Ont., Canada L6W 1M6

The Cat Fanciers' Association, Inc.
1309 Allaire Avenue
Ocean, NJ 07712

The Cat Fanciers' Federation, Inc.
9509 Montgomery Road
Cincinnati, OH 45242

The International Cat Association, Inc.
P.O. Box 2684
Harlingen, TX 78551

Index

Color photos are indicated in **bold face**.

Index